ETHNIC CHRONOLOGY SERIES
NUMBER 2

Blacks in America
1492-1970

A Chronology & Fact Book

Compiled and edited by
Irving J. Sloan

1971
OCEANA PUBLICATIONS, INC.
DOBBS FERRY, NEW YORK

Library of Congress Cataloging in Publication Data

Sloan, Irving J
    Blacks in America, 1492-1970.
    (Ethnic chronology series)
    First -2d ed. published under title: The
American Negro; a chronology and fact book.
    Bibliography: p.
    "Discography; Afro-American folk music in
the United States": p.
    1. Negroes--History--Chronology. I. Title.
II. Series.
E185.S57   1971   973'.04'96073   76-170977
ISBN 0-379-00262-0

© Copyright 1971 by Oceana Publications, Inc.

All rights reserved. No part of this publication may be reproduced or transmitted in any form or by any means, electronic or mechanical, including photocopy, recording, xerography, or any information storage and retrieval system, without permission in writing from the publisher.

Manufactured in the United States of America

To John Harmon,
whose work in Black history
is an inspiration.

CONTENTS

Introduction	vii
Chronology	1
Selected Bibliography on the Afro-American	69
Libraries with Black-American History & Literature Collections	75
Excerpts from Three Landmark Civil Rights Executive Orders	77
An Outline of Afro-American History	80
Discography - Afro-American Folk Music in the United States	93
Predominately Black Colleges and Universities	97
State Agencies with Civil Rights Responsibilities	100
Major Black American Organizations	107
Black American Publications	111
Museums and Monuments of Afro-American Interest	116
Selected Quotations	118
Black Members of the Congress of the United States	128
Statistical Abstract of the Afro-American in the United States	131
Name Index	160

INTRODUCTION

No one can measure the influence or the impact of history on the minds of men. It is certain, however, that the kind of historical treatment --or the lack of it--which the Negro in America has received under the guise of "historical scholarship" has made no small contribution in establishing and perpetuating one of our society's most serious problems: racial discrimination. For the fact is that by omission and commission the history of the American Negro has served to reinforce notions among whites of their superiority and among Negroes of their inferiority.

Dr. John Hope Franklin has distinguished "between what has actually happened and what those who have written history have said has happened." He goes on to hail the changes that have occurred in the writing of the history of the Negro in recent years. Indeed, these changes are even more dramatic than the very events themselves that the writers have been describing. "For the first time in the history of the United States, there is a striking resemblance between what historians are writing and what has actually happened in the history of the American Negro."

This small volume presents chronologically and factually the broad sweep of American Negro history. There is no attempt here to amplify or to interpret. For the most part, a book of this nature serves as a quick, handy and, hopefully, reliable reference work. Having located a person or event of interest, the reader can seek out the full story in any number of books which are filling the shelves of literature on Negro life and history.

Compact as the present work is, one can yet come to have an appreciation of the background and the contribution of the Negro in American life by surveying its contents.

The reader will learn at once that Negro history in America does not begin with the first cargo of slaves which was landed in Jamestown in 1619. It begins with the very beginning of American history with the coming of the European explorers. Scholars, indeed, contend that Columbus' pilot was a Negro. But in any case there is no historical doubt that the discoverer of the Pacific Ocean, Balboa, brought with him 30 Negroes whose assistance was invaluable. Cortez was accompanied by a Negro, who, finding in his rations of rice some grains of wheat, planted them as an experiment and thereby introduced wheat raising in the Western Hemisphere. Negroes participated in the exploration of Guatemala and the conquest of

INTRODUCTION

Chile, Peru, and Venezuela. Negroes were with Ayllon in 1526 in his expedition from the Florida Peninsula northward and took a part in the establishment of the settlement of San Miguel, near what is now Jamestown, Virginia. Negroes accompanied Navarez on his ill-fated adventure in 1526 and continued with Cabeza de Vaca, his successor, through what is now the southwestern part of the United States. There Estevancio, a Negro, discovered Cibola, "the seven cities" of the Zuni Indians. Matthew A. Henson, the last to appear in the role of explorer, was chosen by Commodore Perry to accompany him to the North Pole.

The first important contribution of the Negro to the development of America was labor. First as indentured servants and then after being debased to the status of slaves, Negroes supplied the demand for labor demanded by the expansion of trade in the commercial revolution of the modern era. Negroes cleared the forests of the Southland, drained the swamps, prepared the soil for the production of its staples, and dug from the earth nuggets of precious metals. In all sections of America appeared Negro mechanics and artisans, using the skill which was natural to the African even in his native land. These Negro workers shod horses, cast farming implements, made vehicles, constructed boats, and built railroads.

At the same time the Negro showed inventive genius in producing labor-saving devices. Negroes assisted Eli Whitney in his experiments with the cotton gin and McCormick with his reaper. James Forten perfected a machine for handling sails; Henry Blair patented two corn harvesters; Granville T. Woods stimulated industry with his electrical patents; Elijah McCoy brought machinery nearer to perfection with his lubricating devices; Norbert Rillieux revolutionized the manufacture of sugar with his vacuum pan; and Jan E. Matzeliger revolutionized the shoe industry with the lasting device for making shoes with machinery.

While helping to develop the country, the Negro has done his share in defending it. As this Chronology relates again and again, the Negro has acquitted himself with honor in all American wars. They served with the Colonial forces and helped shape the destiny of America. They followed the British standard during the Seven Years War until Montcalm was vanquished by Wolfe on the Plains of Abraham, thereby making English institutions possible in America.

In the American Revolution some 5,000 Negroes fought on the American side with distinction. Negroes were honored as heroes at Bunker Hill and Stony Point. George Washington praised the Negro soldier. Even more fulsome praise was given the Negro soldier by Andrew Jackson after the Battle of New Orleans in 1815; for during the War of 1812 Negroes also fought with impressive distinction.

The great social and political issue of the years following was the question of slavery in 19th century America. Negro newspapers, such as <u>Freedom's Journal</u> and <u>Walker's Appeal</u>, and Negro leaders, such as Douglass, Garnet, Ward and Pennington, were in the forefront of the abolition movement which brought the nation in the direction of freedom and equality for all.

The Civil War began as a war to save the Union and succeeded also in destroying slavery. Again the Negro participated in promoting democracy in America. Over two hundred thousand Negroes fought with the Union forces. History confirms the deeds of heroism performed by individual Negro soldiers as well as the significant contribution they made to final victory in terms of numbers alone.

The achievements of the Negro in the theatre, literature, music and the arts through the present day are too familiar to warrant recapitulation here. His role in the wars this country has fought and still fights in this century are also well-known if not always well-recognized. Our Chronology here records all this.

What is perhaps most significant and exciting is to note how in the last decade the events and the people involved in present-day Negro history in the making are largely related to the Negroes' struggle on their own behalf for full equality in American society. Coupled with this series of events is the ever-increasing "firsts" among Negroes--the "first" Negro to appear with the Metropolitan Opera; the "first" Negro to enter the Major Leagues in baseball; the "first" Negro to enter a Southern state university, and on and on and on.

And as we see Negroes enter politics and public office our knowledge of Negro history will serve as reassuring evidence that they bring to American public life a background of positive achievements when given the opportunity. During the Reconstruction, contrary to biased and now generally repudiated "history," the Negro gave a good account of himself as a citizen and as a statesman. The majority of the Negro leaders of that day advocated high ideals. The participation of the Negro in the affairs of the Government was denounced and opposed from the very beginning; but despite the mire of corruption into which the Negroes were drawn by the white men who profited at the expense of the freedmen, the Negro demonstrated his capacity for citizenship and his right to all the honors within the gift of the United States. Indeed, the Negro had never imposed upon government such colossal evidences of corruption and scandal as the "credit mobilier," the "whiskey ring," the "Tweed ring" and many others which were recorded throughout the country during the same period.

INTRODUCTION

It is the very aim of a book like this to make some small contribution toward setting down the historical achievements and therefore historical truths concerning such a large part of our American people, the Negro. In proposing this, one need not suggest that we learn less about the great leaders and episodes already recognized and honored in American history. It only means that we include in our knowledge the role of the Negro in our history. Having that knowledge will give us the understanding that the Negroes' long "advance from slavery to freedom and from freedom to equality has significantly involved and affected the lives of millions of Americans of all races and all generations." Such an understanding will make it possible to accept Negro fellow citizens as equals-and this, after all, is what the most critical issue of our democratic society is all about today.

CHRONOLOGY

1442	First African slave brought to Lisbon, Portugal.
1492	Pedro Alonzo Nino, said by many scholars to have been a Negro, arrived with Columbus as one of his pilots. Oct. 12.
1513	Balboa's expedition to the Pacific included thirty Blacks who were instrumental in clearing the way between two oceans. April.
1517	Bishop Las Casas influenced the Spanish government to allow Spaniards to import twelve Negroes each to encourage immigration to the New World.
1526	The first slave revolt took place in the first United States settlement which contained slaves--an area in present-day South Carolina. April 22.
1538	Estevanico (Little Stephen), a Black explorer, led expedition from Mexico and discovered Arizona and New Mexico.
1539	Blacks accompanied De Soto on his journey to the Mississippi.
1540	The second settler in the state of Alabama was a Black who was with De Soto's expedition. Liking the land, he settled among the Indians.
1562	John Hawkins carried slaves from Portuguese Africa to Spanish America.
1565	Blacks were with Mendez in founding St. Augustine, Florida.
1619	A Dutch ship anchored at Jamestown, Virginia, with a cargo of "twenty Negras"--thus began Black history in English America. Aug.
1620	The first public school for Negroes and Indians in Virginia was established.
1624	William Tucker was the first Black child born and baptized in English America at Jamestown, Virginia.
1638	First Black slaves were brought into New England.

1641	Massachusetts was the first colony to recognize slavery as a legal institution.
1644	Marriage of Antony van Angola and Lucie d'Angola was the first in Negro life to be recorded in America on Manhattan Island.
1645	Voyage of the <u>Rainbowe</u>, the first American slave ship.
1661	First individual petition of a Black for his freedom addressed to the colony of New Netherland was granted.
1662	Virginia enacted a statute making slavery hereditary, following the status of the mother.
1663	The first major slave rebellion in colonial America took place in Gloucester, Virginia.
1664	Maryland passed a law preventing marriages between English women and Negroes; several of the colonies followed suit soon thereafter.
1671	Maryland passed Act declaring that conversion of slaves to Christianity did not affect their slave status.
1672	The King of England chartered the Royal African Company which came to dominate the world slave trade.
1688	Quakers of Germantown, Pennsylvania, made the first formal protest against slavery in the Western hemisphere. Feb. 18.
1704	Elias Nau, a Frenchman, opened the first school for Blacks in New York City.
1705	Virginia enacted a law permitting owners to list people as property.
1712	Early slave revolt in New York City. April 7. Pennsylvania passed first legislation to prevent importation of slaves.
1713	Anthony Benezet, a teacher of Blacks and leading abolitionist in Pennsylvania, born.
1715	Francisco Xavier de Luna Victoria was the first Black to become bishop in America (Panama).

CHRONOLOGY

1720	Jupiter Hammon of Long Island, the first Black American writer, was born in Africa.
1731	Benjamin Banneker, colonial mathematician and astronomer, was born near Baltimore, Maryland. Nov. 9.
1733	Samuel Sewall published the first anti-slavery tract which appeared in the colonies, "The Selling of Joseph."
1741	A serious slave revolt in New York City resulted in the hanging of eighteen Blacks. March-April.
1745	A Black, Jean Baptiste Pointe Du Saible, who established a trading post which later became the city of Chicago, was born in Haiti.
1746	Toussaint L'ouverture, revolutionary leader of Haiti, born. May 20.
1747	Absalom Jones, first Black minister ordained in America, born a slave in Sussex, Delaware.
1748	Prince Hall, successful businessman and founder of Negro Free Masonry, born.
1750	Crispus Attucks, first martyr of the American Revolution, escaped from his master in Framingham, Massachusetts. Sept. 30.
1753	Scipio Moorhead, earliest known Black artist, born. Lemuel Haynes, first Negro to serve as pastor in white congregation in the United States, born. July 18.
1756	John Woolman began his campaign against slavery. May 12.
1758	Frances Williams, first Black college graduate in Western hemisphere, published Latin poems. April 17.
1759	Paul Cuffee, business leader and philanthropist, born. Jan. 17.
1760	Richard Allen, founder and bishop of the African Methodist Church, born a slave near Philadelphia. Feb. 14.
1761	Phillis Wheatley, poetess of the American Revolutionary period, arrived in Boston harbor on a slave ship.

BLACKS IN AMERICA

1761 — Jupiter Hammon published "An Evening Thought." Dec. 15.

1762 — James Derham, the first recognized Black medical doctor in America, born in Philadelphia.

1768 — Rev. James Varick, first Superintendent and bishop of the African Methodist Episcopal Zion Church, born in New York City.

1770 — Crispus Attucks was the first of the five men to be killed in the Boston Massacre. March 5.
Anthony Benezet opened school for Negroes in Philadelphia. June 28.

1772 — Lord Mansfield handed down his decision in the Somerset case against the existence of slavery on English soil. This case stimulated requests for legislative action against slavery in New England. June 22.

1773 — George Leile and Andrew Bryan organized the first Negro Baptist Church in Savannah, Georgia.
Bill Richmond, father of modern prize fighting, born in Staten Island.
Jean Baptiste Point du Saible, first permanent settler in Chicago, purchased the house and land of Jean Baptiste Millet at "Old Peoria Fort."
Massachusetts slaves petitioned the state legislature for their freedom. Jan. 6.

1774 — Continental Congress voted an agreement not to import any slaves after December 1.

1775 — Bejamin Franklin was elected president upon the establishment of the first abolition society organized in America by the Quakers in Philadelphia. April 14.
Black soldiers fought in the Battle of Bunker Hill. Peter Salem, who shot down Major Pitcairn, was one of the heroes of the day. June 17.
Continental Congress passed a resolution barring Blacks from the American Revolutionary Army. Oct. 13.
Lord Dunmore, royal governor of Virginia, issued a proclamation offering freedom to all male slaves who joined the British forces. Nov. 7.
General George Washington, alarmed by the response to Dunmore's Proclamation, ordered recruiting officers to accept free Blacks. December 31.

CHRONOLOGY

Thomas Paine wrote his first published essay in the cause of abolition in a Pennsylvania newspaper.
The first lodge of Negro Free Masons was founded by Prince Hall. July 3.

1776   Continental Congress approved Washington's action of permitting free Blacks to enlist in the Revolutionary Army. Jan. 16.
Mason-Dixon line named for two English surveyors. Feb. 18.
Phillis Wheatley was invited by General Washington to visit him at his headquarters in Cambridge, Mass., so that he might express appreciation for her poem in his honor. Feb. 28.
The Declaration of Independence was adopted without section denouncing slave trade, one of the original grievances against the British king. July 4.
Two Blacks, Prince Whipple and Oliver Cromwell, were with General Washington on Christmas day when he crossed the Delaware. Dec. 25.
Gabriel Prosser, leader of historic slave revolt in Virginia, born a slave.

1777   Vermont was the first state to abolish slavery. July 2.

1778   Four hundred Blacks held off fifteen hundred British in the Battle of Rhode Island. Aug. 28.
More than three thousand Blacks fought in the Revolutionary War.

1779   Twenty slaves petitioned the New Hampshire legislature to abolish slavery. Nov. 12.
Anthony Wayne's victory at Stony Point made possible by the spying of "Pompey," a Black soldier.

1780   Pennsylvania passed a law for the gradual abolition of slavery.
Lott Carey, an early Negro Baptist missionary, born.
First license to a Black preacher granted.

1783   Revolutionary War soldiers, "The Black Regiment," disbanded at Saratoga, N.Y. June 13.
Treaty of Paris, Article VII, promised return to Americans all Negro slaves.

1784   North Carolina answered petition of Edward Griffin, Black Revolutionary soldier, commended his meritorious service, and freed him. May 4.
Phillis Wheatley died in Boston. Dec. 5.

1785   Constitutional Convention approved three clauses protecting slavery. Sept. 17.
David Walker, first Black to attack slavery in published writings, born in Wilmington, North Carolina. Sept. 28.

1786   Arthur Tappan, leading white abolitionist, born. May 22.

1787   Congress added a provision to the Northwest Ordinance forbidding slavery in the territory covered by the Ordinance. July 13.
First free school in New York City, the African Free School, opened. Nov. 1.

1788   Andrew Bryan ordained the first pastor of the First African Baptist Church organized in Savannah, Georgia. Jan. 19-20.

1789   Josiah Henson, the model for Harriet Beecher Stowe's "Uncle Tom," of the famed novel, was born a slave in Maryland; he later became a leading abolitionist orator. June 15.

1790   The Pennsylvania Abolition Society petitioned Congress to abolish slavery. Feb. 3.
Samuel Cornish born in Delaware.
First United States census showed Black population of 757,181, with 59,557 free.

1791   Benjamin Banneker was appointed, at the suggestion of Thomas Jefferson, to serve as member of commission headed by L'enfant to lay out plans for the city of Washington in District of Columbia.

1792   Antoine Blanc founded the first Negro Catholic sisterhood in the United States. Oct. 11.

1793   Benjamin Lundy, colonizationist, born. Jan. 4.
First fugitive slave law enacted by Congress, making it criminal offense to protect a fugitive slave. Feb. 12.
Eli Whitney invented cotton gin which influenced mass importation of Blacks and thereby strengthened slaver as an institution.

CHRONOLOGY

	Dr. Benjamin Rush of Philadelphia sought the aid of the Blacks of the city to administer medicines and care for the sick during yellow fever epidemic. It was believed that Blacks were immune.
1794	Richard Allen organized African Methodist Episcopal Church. June 10. St. Thomas Church, Philadelphia, first Episcopal Negro Congregation, organized. Oct. 12.
1796	Zion Methodist Church organized in New York City.
1797	First petition by Blacks was submitted to Congress protesting a North Carolina law requiring Blacks who were freed by their Quaker masters to be returned to the state and to their slavery status. The petition was rejected. Jan. 30. Sojourner Truth, leading abolitionist figure in Black history, born a slave in Hurley, New York.
1798	Thaddeus Koscuisko, Polish patriot, left will providing for education of Blacks. May 5. James P. Beckwourth, scout for General Fremont and noted pioneer and explorer of the West, born in Virginia. Levi Coffin, organizer of the underground railroad, born. Oct. 28.
1799	Alexander Pushkin, Russian Black poet, born in Moscow.
1800	The free Blacks of Philadelphia presented a petition to Congress opposing the slave trade, the Fugitive Act of 1793, and the institution of slavery itself. Jan. 2. Gabriel Prosser, a Virginia slave, was betrayed in his plot to lead thousands of slaves in an attack on Richmond, Virginia. Dozens of slaves were imprisoned or hanged on the spot, and Gabriel himself was publicly hanged. Aug. 30. John Brown born in Torrington, Connecticut. May 9. James Derham began practicing medicine in New Orleans. Nat Turner, destined to lead another major slave rebellion, born a slave in Southhampton County, Virginia. Oct. 2.
1802	Alexander Dumas, French novelist of Black extraction, born in France.
1803	Lunsford Lane, noted lecturer for the American Anti-Slavery Society, born a slave in Raleigh, North Carolina. Toussaint L'ouverture, slave leader of Haitian Revolution, died. April 27.

1804	The Ohio legislature enacted the first of the "Black Laws" which restricted rights and movements of Negroes in the North; other Northern states soon passed similar legislation. Jan. 5.
1805	Benjamin Banneker died. Oct. 9. William E. Dodge, proponent of Black education, born.
1806	Maria Weston Chapman, abolitionist, born. July 25. Norbert Rillieux, inventor and scientist, born in New Orleans.
1807	British Parliament abolished the slave trade. March 25. Ira F. Aldridge, one of the greatest Shakespearean actors of his time, was born in New York City. Charles Bennet Ray, minister, editor, lecturer, organizer, and abolitionist, born in Massachusetts.
1808	Federal law barring the African slave trade went into effect. Jan. 1.
1809	Abraham Lincoln born in Harden County, Kentucky. Feb. 12. James W. C. Pennington, leader in the Free Negro Convention Movement which outlined an ideology and tactics for the Black protest in the 19th century, born a slave in Washington County, Maryland. Abyssinian Baptist Church organized in New York City. July 5.
1810 February	Charles Lenox Remond, leader of the American Anti-Slavery Society, born in Massachusetts. Feb. 1. Thomy Lafon, philanthropist who supported the American Anti-Slavery society and the underground railroad, born in New Orleans.
August	Theodore Parker, liberal minister, born. Aug. 24.
October	Cassius M. Clay, Kentucky emancipationist, born. Oct. 19. David Ruggles, founder of Mirror of Liberty--first Black periodical--born.
1811 January	Charles Sumner, great New England advocate of Black rights, born. Jan. 6.
February	Rev. Daniel A. Payne, African Methodist Episcopalian, who established Union Seminary near Columbus, Ohio, born. Feb. 24.
June	Harriet Beecher Stowe, author of Uncle Tom's Cabin, born. June 14.

CHRONOLOGY

1812   Martin R. Delaney, newspaper editor and author, Union Army Major, born. May 6.
George Washington, pioneer, humanitarian and founder of Centralia, Washington, born a slave. Aug. 15.
The Union Church of Africans, organized and incorporated. Sept. 25.
Bishop Richard Allen and Reverend Absalom Jones were requested to help organize defenses for Philadelphia against the British who had recently attacked Washington.
John Johnson, one of many Blacks who served in the Navy on the Great Lakes during the War of 1812, was described by his commander after his death in a naval battle: "When America has such tars, she has little to fear from tyrants of the ocean."

1813   Henry Ward Beecher, promoter for equal rights, born. June 24.
James McCune Smith born of slaves in New York City.

1814   Daniel Reaves Goodloe, North Carolinan emancipationist, born. May 28.
General Andrew Jackson appealed to free Blacks to fight as part of the militia. Sept. 21.
New York legislature authorized the raising of two Black regiments. As a result 2000 Blacks were enlisted and sent to the army at Sacketts Harbor. Oct. 24.

1815   Henry Highland Garnet, minister, abolitionist, and diplomat, born a slave in Kent County, Maryland. Dec. 23.
Myrtilla Miner, founder of Miner's Teachers College, born. March 4.

1816   The African Methodist Episcopal Church became independent of jurisdictional control by higher all-white bodies. April 9.
Peter Salem, hero of Bunker Hill, died. Aug. 16.
John Jones, "the most prominent citizen of Chicago" during his lifetime, born in Greene County, North Carolina.
The Seminole Wars led by General Andrew Jackson began with an attack on a fort in western Florida which contained hundreds of runaway slaves living among the Creek and Seminole Indians who occupied it.
Bishop Daniel Wayne, reformer and educator, born.

1817   Free Blacks in the large cities held protest meetings against the American Colonization Society's efforts to "exile us from the land of our nativity." Jan.

Frederick Douglass, orator, editor and statesman, was born a slave in Talbot County, Maryland. Feb. 14.
Victor Sejour, Black Creole poet and dramatist, born. June 2.
The American Colonization Society was organized under the leadership of John C. Calhoun and Henry Clay. Its purpose was to transport free Negroes to Africa. Dec. 28.
Samuel Ringgold Ward, the "Black Daniel Webster," was born in Maryland; he was one of the most noted Black abolitionists. Oct. 17.
James Forten, Black abolitionist, was chairman of the First Negro Convention held in Philadelphia. Jan. 23.
Paul Cuffee, Black shipbuilder and African colonizer, died.

1818　　Philadelphia free Blacks established the Pennsylvania Augustine Society, "for the education of people of colour."
St. Philip's Episcopal Church was opened for Blacks in New York City.
Absolom Jones died. Feb. 13.
Charles L. Reason, Black writer, born. July 21.

1820　　Missouri Compromise enacted; prohibited slavery north of Missouri. March 3.
Harriet Tubman born a slave in Dorchester County, Maryland.
The American Colonization Society founded Liberia, a Negro Republic in West Africa.

1821　　Lott Carey, minister and pioneer leader in Liberia, sailed for that country. Jan. 23.
African Methodist Episcopal Zion Church founded in New York City. June 21.
William Still, author of Underground Railroad and leading underground spokesman, born in New Jersey. Oct. 7.
Alexander Crummell, one of the most highly educated Blacks of his time, born.

1822　　Denmark Vesey planned one of the most extensive slave revolts ever recorded. The plot was betrayed and Vesey together with thirty-six others were executed. July 2.
Hiram R. Revels, first Black United States Senator, was born free in Fayetteville, North Carolina. Sept. 27.
Rev. John Gloucester, first Black minister of a Presbyterian church, died.

CHRONOLOGY

1823	Thomas Wentworth Higginson, white commander of Black soldiers, born.
1825	Frances Ellen Watkins Harper, poet and orator, born in Baltimore, Maryland.
1826	James Madison Bell, poet and abolitionist, born free at Gallipolis, Ohio. April 3. John Russworm was the first Black to graduate from an American college when he received his degree from Bowdoin College, Maine. Ira F. Aldridge made his London debut in Othello; he never returned to America and became the most famous Shakespearean actor of his time on the continent.
1827	Slavery was officially abolished in New York State. July 4. Freedom's Journal, the first Black newspaper, was published in New York City by John Russworm and Samuel Cornish. March 16.
1828	Lott Carey, first missionary to Liberia, died. April 1.
1829	Walker's Appeal, militant anti-slavery pamphlet published by David Walker, was distributed throughout the country and aroused the Blacks and provoked slave-holders. Jan. 18. John Mercer Langston born. Dec. 14.
1830	James Augustine Healy, the first Black Roman Catholic bishop in America, born to an Irish planter and a Negro slave on a plantation near Macon, Georgia. April 6. S. R. Lowry, religious educator, born. Dec. 9. United States Bureau of the Census reported 3,777 Black heads of families who owned slaves; most of these Blacks lived in Louisiana, Maryland, Virginia, North Carolina, South Carolina, and Virginia. Dan Rice, famous white "blackface" minstrel began performing "Jump Jim Crow" song-dance--from which song the words "Jim Crow" came to be applied to legal segregation.
1831	The first issue of the Liberator was published by William Lloyd Garrison. Jan. 1. Nat Turner led the greatest slave rebellion in the United States in Virginia; the whole South was thrown into panic and more than one hundred and sixty whites and Negroes were killed before the revolt ended. Aug. 21-23.

Bishop John Walden, advocate of Black education, born. Feb. 11.
Nat Turner executed. Nov. 11.

1832
Joseph P. Rainey, Black Congressman from South Carolina, born. June 21.
Dr. Edward W. Blyden, distinguished scholar and diplomat, president of Liberia College, born. Aug. 3.
The New England Anti-Slavery Society was established by twelve whites at the African Baptist Church in Boston.

1833
Oberlin College opened and admitted Blacks at the outset.
Frederick Douglass escaped from his master and fled to New York.
The Philadelphia Negro Library was organized.
Henry Macneil Turner, a bishop of the African Methodist Church and colonizationist, was free-born in Abbeville, South Carolina.
The American Anti-Slavery Society was organized in Philadelphia by Negro and white abolitionists. Dec. 4.

1834
Slavery abolished in the British Empire. Aug. 1.
Henry Blair was the first Black to receive a patent for an invention, a corn harvester. Oct. 14.
South Carolina enacted a law prohibiting the teaching of free or slave Black children.
Black youth leaders formed the Garrison Literary and Benevolent Association of New York in order "to begin, in early life, to assist each other to alleviate the afflicted. . ."
The first school for Blacks in Cincinnati, paid for by themselves, was opened.
Bishop Isaac Lane, founder of Lane College in Jackson, Tennessee, born.
Anti-abolition riot broke out in Philadelphia and continued for three days and nights.

1835
Fifth National Negro Convention resolved to recommend that Blacks remove the word "African" from the names of their institutions and organizations, and also to abandon the use of the word "colored" when referring to themselves. June 1-5.
John Greenleaf Whittier published his poem, "My Countrymen in Chains."
New York City Blacks formed a bigilance committee to prevent kidnapping of Blacks and to assist fugitive slaves.
William Whipper helped to found the American Moral Reform Society, a Black abolitionist group.

CHRONOLOGY

1836   Theodore S. Wright, first Black to receive a degree from a theological seminary in the United States (Princeton). Nov. 5.

1837   P. S. B. Pinchback, Black Reconstructionist statesman in Louisiana, born. May 10.
Robert Gould Shaw, Colonel of the 54th Massachusetts Union Regiment, first Black company sent from the free states, born in Boston of a "proper" Bostonian family which was deeply committed to the cause of Black freedom. Oct. 10.
Elijah P. Lovejoy was murdered by a mob in Alton, Illinois, when he refused to stop publishing anti-slavery material. Nov. 7.
James M. Smith, University of Glasgow graduate, conducted pioneer work in the scientific study of race.
William Whipper published "An Address on Non-Resistance to Offensive Aggression"--an article written twelve years before Thoreau's famous essay on non-violence, and more than 125 years before the career of Martin Luther King, Jr.

1838   The first Black periodical, <u>Mirror of Freedom</u>, began publishing in New York City. Aug. 30.
Frederick Douglass escaped from slavery in Baltimore. Sept. 3.
Charles Lenox Remond became first Black lecturer employed by an anti-slavery society.

1839   Robert Smalls, Civil War hero and Reconstructionist Congressman, born in Beaufort, South Carolina. April 5.
Lunsford Lane of North Carolina made the only abolition speech before a southern audience. April 30.
Benjamin Lundy died. Aug. 22.
Liberty Party, first anti-slavery political party, organized. Nov. 13.
Whites burned the Black section of Pittsburgh.
The most famous slave revolt aboard a slave ship took place on the Spanish slaver the <u>Amistad</u>. John Quincy Adams, at the age of 73 and out of law practice more than thirty years, argued the case before the United States Supreme Court. Cinque, the young African leader, and his fellow crewmen were freed by the Court.

1840   James M. Turner, a Lincoln University founder, born in Jefferson City, Missouri. May 16.

1841   Blanche Kelso Bruce, only Black to serve full term in United States Senate, born a slave at Prince Edward County, Virginia. March 1.

President Tyler sent a message to Congress dealing with the suppression of the slave trade. June 1.
Frederick Douglass became lecturer for the Massachusetts Anti-Slavery Society. Aug.
James M. Townsend, first Black to serve as member of Indiana Legislature, born. Aug. 18.
Slave trader "Creole" was scene of slave revolt. Slaves took over ship and sailed to Bahamas where they were given asylum and freedom. Nov.

1842　Robert Brown Elliott, Reconstruction Congressman from South Carolina, born. Aug. 11.
Charlie Smith, last known slave brought to America, born in Liberia.
James Forten died in Philadelphia.
Capture of George Latimore in Boston precipitated the first of several famous fugitive slave cases which embittered North and South. Boston abolitionists raised enough money to purchase Latimore from his master. Nov. 17.

1843　Sojourner Truth, first Black woman to become lecturer against slavery, left New York and began her work as an abolitionist. June 1.
Henry Highland Garnet made controversial speech at the National Convention of Colored Men in Buffalo calling for a slave revolt and a general strike. Aug. 22.
Blacks participated in a national political gathering for the first time at a meeting of the Liberty Party convention in Buffalo, New York. Aug. 30.

1844　James Beckwourth discovered a pass through the coast range to the Pacific Ocean which was named for him, <u>Beckwourth Pass</u>. April 26.
Elijah J. McCoy, inventor (lubricating cup), born. May 2.
Charles Nash, Congressman from Louisiana, born. May 23.

1845　Macon B. Allen was the first Black formally admitted to the bar when he passed the examination at Worcester, Massachusetts. May 3.
<u>Narrative of Frederick Douglass</u> published.
Publication of <u>Les Cenelles</u>, in French and English, an anthology of poetry by Negro poets of New Orleans.
Frederick Douglass delivered the commencement address at Western Reserve College which was one of the first Black attempts to refute racism scientifically.

CHRONOLOGY 15

1847	Frederick Douglass began to publish his own newspaper, the North Star. Dec. 3. William Alexander Leidesdorff, Black businessman, launched the first steamboat to sail in San Francisco Bay; he later built the first hotel in that city. Dred Scott case initiated in St. Louis Circuit Court. June 30.
1848	Negro blacksmith Lewis Temple invented a Toggle harpoon which became the standard harpoon of the American whaling industry. William and Ellen Craft escaped from slavery in Georgia in one of the most dramatic escapes of the period. Dec. 26.
1849	Harriet Tubman escaped from slavery in Maryland. July. Archibald H. Grimke, Harvard Law School graduate and author of biographies of Charles Sumner and William Lloyd Garrison, born near Charleston, South Carolina. Aug. 17. Benjamin Roberts filed the first school integration suit on behalf of his daughter who had been denied admission to the white schools in Boston. The Supreme Court of Massachusetts rejected the suit and established the "separate but equal" doctrine. "Blind Tom," the greatest musical prodigy of his time, born a slave in Georgia.
1850	Fugitive Slave Law passed by Congress as part of the Compromise of 1850; it offered federal officers a fee for captured slaves. Sept. 18.
1851	William C. Nell published Services of Colored Americans in the Wars of 1776 and 1812, the first full-length study of the American Black. Walter H. Brooks, distinguished clergyman, born. Aug. 30.
1852	First edition of Uncle Tom's Cabin published. March 20. Napoleon issued a decree against the slave trade. March 29.
1853	First Black YMCA established in Washington, D.C. Jan. 3. William Wells Brown wrote Clotel, the first novel by a Black American. Publication of Solomon Northrup's Narrative of a Slave, one of the most famous of the many narratives written by fugitive slaves telling their stores.

1854   Lincoln University, the first Black college, was chartered as Ashmond Institute in Chester, Pennsylvania. Jan. 1.
August Tolon, first Black Catholic priest to serve in the United States, was born in Battle Creek, Missouri. April 1.
Lucey C. Laney, founder of Haines Institute in Augusta, Georgia, born. April 13.
Kansas-Nebraska Act repealed the Missouri Compromise and opened Northern territory to slavery. May 30.
Anthony Burns was returned to slavery in Virginia in spite of an attempt by Boston citizens to purchase his freedom for $1200. June 3.
The Republican Party was created by Free Soilers and Whigs as well as Democrats who were opposed to the extension of slavery.

1855   Black troops mustered into Confederate service. March 24.

1856   Booker T. Washington born a slave in Franklin County, Virginia. April 5.
Granville T. Woods, inventor of industrial appliances, born. April 23.
Wilberforce University founded by Methodist Episcopal Church. Aug. 30

1857   Dred Scott decision by the United States Supreme Court opened federal territory to slavery and denied citzenship to Black Americans. May 6.
Dred Scott and his family were freed by the new owner, Taylor Blow. May 26.

1858   Daniel Hale Williams, called the "Father of Negro Hospitals," born in Hollidayburg, Pennsylvania. Jan. 18.
Twelve whites and thirty-four Negroes attended John Brown's anti-slavery convention in Chatham, Canada. May 8.
Charles W. Chestnutt, Black pioneer novelist, born. June 20.
Lecompton, Kansas constitution, sanctioning slavery, rejected. Aug. 2.
William Wells Brown published <u>The Escape</u>, first play written by an American Black.

1859   Henry O. Tanner, world famous artist, born in Pittsburgh. June 21.
John Brown met for last time with Frederick Douglass at an old quarry in Chambersburg, Pennsylvania. Aug. 19.
John Brown raided Harper's Ferry. Oct. 16.

CHRONOLOGY 17

The last slave ship, <u>Clothilde</u>, landed its cargo of slaves at Mobile, Alabama.
Samuel Cornish, one of the first men to approach the race problem from an economic point of view, died.
John Brown hanged at Charles Town, West Virginia. Dec. 2.

1860   George Washington Carver born in Diamond Grove, Missouri.
Abraham Lincoln elected President. Nov. 6.
South Carolina declared herself an "independent commonwealth." Dec. 18.

1861   Robert Smalls (Union Navy pilot) watching preparations for the attack on Fort Sumter, said "this, boys, is the dawn of freedom for our race." April 10.
Confederates attacked Fort Sumter. April 12.
Lincoln issued proclamation calling for 75,000 volunteers from the states. April 15.
Loyal Black volunteers were not accepted when the first call for troops was made.
Clara Barton with five Black girls gave aid to the wounded in the passage through Baltimore. April 21.
General B. F. Butler refused to return three escaped slaves as they were "contraband of war." May 24.
General George B. McClellan, Ohio Department, issued orders to suppress any Black attempts at insurrection. May 26.
Black Mass Meeting offered to raise an army of 50,000 men and that the women would serve as nurses, etc. May 31.
Hampton Institute's first day, with Mary S. Peake, as the first Black teacher. Aug. 17.
The Secretary of the Navy authorized the enlistment of Black slaves later in the year. Sept. 25.

1862   President Lincoln recommended to Congress gradual, compensated emancipation. March 6.
United States Senate passed bill abolishing slavery in the District of Columbia. April 4.
Robert Smalls, Black pilot, sailed armed Confederate steamer, the <u>Planter</u>, out of Charleston, South Carolina, and presented her to the United States Navy. May 13.
Liberia recognized as a free nation by the United States. June 3.
Lincoln recommended aid to states abolishing slavery. July 14.

The first regular colored troops were enlisted at Leavenworth, Kansas. July 17.
Anthony Burns, Baptist clergyman whose capture as a fugitive slave caused a riot in Boston, died. July 27.
Charlotte Forten, Black poet and teacher, arrived in St. Helena, South Carolina, to teach Blacks. Oct. 29.
First African Methodist Episcopal Church established at New Bern, North Carolian. Dec. 27.

1863
President Lincoln signed the Emancipation Proclamation. Jan. 1.
The War Department authorized Massachusetts governor to recruit Black troops. The Fifty-fourth Massachusetts Volunteers was the first Black regiment raised in the North. Jan. 26.
Two Black infantry regiments, First and Second, South Carolina, captured and occupied Jacksonville, Florida, causing panic along the Southern seabord. March 10.
Confederate Congress passed resolution which branded Black troops and their officers criminals; thus caputred Black soldiers could be put to death or slavery. May 1.
Eight Black regiments played important role in the seige of Port Hudson which, with the fall of Vicksburg, gave the Union control of the Mississippi River and cut the Confederacy into two sections. July 9.
The New York City Draft Riots were the bloodiest in American history. July 13-17.
The Fifty-fourth Massachusetts Volunteers made a charge on Fort Wagner in Charleston Harbor, South Carolina. At least one member of the all-Black regiment won the Congressional Medal of Honor for his bravery. July 18.
Kelly Miller, author and educator, born. July 18.
Dr. Mary Church Terrell, first president of the National Association of Colored Women, born. Sept. 23.

1864
Famous Battle of Fort Pillow and the massacre of Black troops after its surrender. April 12.
In a duel between USS Kearsage and CSS Alabama off the coast of France, a Black sailor, Joachim Pease, displayed "marked coolness," and won the Congressional Medal of Honor. June 19.
Fugitive slave laws repealed. June 28.
Maryland constitution amended to abolish slavery. July 7.
Although he himself was not certain of actual date, George Washington Carver celebrated his birthday on this date. July 12.

New Orleans Tribune began publishing as the first daily
Black newspaper in French and English. Oct. 14.
Richard B. Harrison, featured actor who created the role of
"De Lawd" in Green Pastures, born. Aug. 28.
Congress passed a bill equalizing for the first time the pay,
arms, equipment and medical services of Black troops.
Charles Young (Colonel), West Point graduate who held the
highest rank in his time, born.
"Blind Boone," John W. Boone, a noted musical prodigy,
born in Miami, Missouri.
First public school system for Blacks opened in the District
of Columbia.

1865   General Lee said that it was "not only expedient but neces-
sary" that the Confederate Army use Black slaves as soldiers.
Jan. 11.
John S. Rock was the first Black to practice before the United
States Supreme Court. Feb. 1.
Henry Highland Garnet was the first Black to preach in the
Capitol delivering a sermon on the abolition of slavery.
Feb. 12.
Congress passed a bill giving freedom to wives and children
of Black soldiers. March 3.
The Freedman's Bureau established by Congress to help the
newly emancipated slaves. March 13.
Abraham Lincoln died from wounds received when shot at
Ford's Theater by actor John Wilkes Booth. April 15.
Two white regiments and a Negro regiment, the 62nd USCT,
fought the last action of the Civil War at White's Ranch,
Texas. Sergeant Crocket, a Black, believed to have been the
last man to shed blood in the War. May 13.
President Andrew Johnson announced his Reconstruction
plan. May 29.
South Carolina abolished slavery. Aug. 27.
Timothy T. Fortune, journalist and founder of the New York
Age, born. Oct. 3.
Congress passed the Thirteenth Amendment which, on rati-
fication, abolished slavery in the United States. Dec. 18.
Fisk University opened. April 20.
Patrick Henry Healy was the first Black to win the Doctor
of Philosophy degree when he passed his final examination
in Louvain, Belgium. July 26.
Matthew A. Henson, Black explorer who accompanied Peary
to the North Pole, born in Charles County, Maryland. Aug-
ust 8.

Edward G. Walker and Charles L. Mitchell were elected to the Massachusetts House of Representatives thus becoming the first Blacks elected to an American legislative assembly.
Ku Klux Klan organized in Tennessee.
Shaw University founded.
Howard University founded as Howard Seminary in Washington, D.C. Nov. 20.

1867   Talladega and Morehouse College opened. Feb.
Peabody Educational Fund established for the South. Feb. 7.
Maggie Lena Walker, the first woman bank president in the United States, born in Richmond, Virginia.
Robert R. Moton, outstanding educator, born. Aug. 26.
William Still led a successful campaign against segregated streetcars in Philadelphia.
Samuel Ringgold Ward died in the British West Indies.

1868   William Edward Burghardt Du Bois born in Great Barrington, Massachusetts. Feb. 23.
Hampton Institute opened. April
Fourteenth Amendment became part of the Constitution. July 28.
John Hope, educator, born. June 2.
Oscar J. Dunn, ex-slave, became Lieutenant Governor of Louisiana, the highest elective office then held by a Black American. June 13.

1869   Will Marion Cook, famed composer, born. Jan. 27.
Jefferson P. Long from Georgia was seated as the first Negro in the House of Representatives.
The American Anti-Slavery Society was dissolved.
Ebenezer Don Carlos Bennett was the first Black to receive an appointment in the diplomatic service when he became Minister to Haiti. April 16.

1870   Fifteenth Amendment adopted, giving the Black the right to vote. March 30.
Thomas Peterson was the first Black to vote in the United States the day after the Fifteenth Amendment was ratified.
Robert S. Abbott, founder of the Chicago Defender, born on St. Simon's Island off the coast of Georgia. Nov. 24.
James W. C. Pennington died.
Freedman's Bureau expired by law.

CHRONOLOGY

1871   James Weldon Johnson, poet, educator, civil rights fighter, first Black consul to Nicaragua, born in Jacksonville, Florida. June 17.
Fisk Jubilee Singers made their first appearances under the direction of George L. White.
Oscar De Priest, first Black Congressman elected from a northern state (Illinois), born.

1872   Booker T. Washington entered Hampton Institute.
Paul Laurence Dunbar, nationally-known poet and short story writer, born in Dayton, Ohio. June 27.
John H. Conyers was the first Black admitted to the United States Naval Academy. Oct. 21.
P.B.S. Pinchback became Acting Governor of Louisiana on the impeachment of the Governor. Dec. 11.
First Black police officer appointed in Chicago.
Charlotte E. Ray, the first Black woman lawyer, graduated from Howard University Law School; she was first woman to graduate from a university law school.
William Still published the records of the fugitive slaves in the classic, <u>Underground Railroad</u>.

1873   Slavery abolished in Puerto Rico. March 23.
John W. Work, musician, Black folk singer expert, born. Aug. 6.
W. C. Handy, "Father of the Blues," born in Florence, Alabama. Nov. 16.
Richard T. Greener, first Black graduate of Harvard University, named professor of metaphysics at the University of South Carolina.

1874   William C. Nell died. May 25.
Patrick Henry Healy, Black inaugurated as President of Georgetown University, oldest Catholic university in the United States. July 31.

1875   Blacks massacred at Hamburg, South Carolina. July 9.
Civil Rights Bill enacted by Congress contained equal accommodations provisions. March 1.
Mary McLeod Bethune, noted educator, born in Mayesville, South Carolina. July 10.
Blanche K. Bruce became a member of the United States Senate from Mississippi, the only Black to serve a full term in the Senate. March 15.
Carter G. Woodson, scholar and historian, born in New Canton, Virginia. Dec. 19.
Booker T. Washington graduated from Hampton Institute.

1876   E. M. Bannister, Black painter, exhibited and received first prize for his "under the Oaks" at the Philadelphia Centennial Exposition. July 4.
Edward A. Bounchet received the Doctor of Philosophy degree in physics at Yale University, the first Black awarded the doctorate by an American university.
"Bert" Williams, described by Billboard as "the greatest comedian on the American stage" in the early 1900's, born in the Bahamas.

1877   Meta Vaux Fuller, noted sculptress of the 19th Century, born June 9.
Henry O. Flipper, born a slave in Georgia, was the first Black graduate from West Point. June 15.
Frederick Doublass appointed Marshal of the District of Columbia by President Rutherford B. Hayes.
Reconstruction ended with the withdrawal of all Union troops from the South.

1879   William Lloyd Garrison died. May 24.
Blanche K. Bruce presided over the United States Senate. Feb. 15.

1881   William Ickins, orator, author and equal rights fighter, born. Jan 15.
Frederick Douglass appointed Recorder of Deeds for the District of Columbia. May 17.
Booker T. Washington began his work at Tuskegee Institute. July 4.

1882   Mrs. Violette A. Johnson, first Black woman admitted to practice before the United States Supreme Court, born. July 16.
Benjamin Brawley, social historian, born. April 22.
Charlotte Hawkins Brown, founder of the Palmer Institute at Sedalia, North Carolina, born.
John F. Slater Fund of one million dollars was created for education and uplifting the Blacks in the South.
Robert Morris, first Black to practice in the courts of the United States, died. Dec. 11.
First Jim Crow railroad car law passed in Tennessee--beginning of modern segregation movement as other Southern states followed.

1883   Shoe lasting machine patented by Jan Matzeliger, American Black inventor. March 20.

Spellman College organized in basement of church in Atlanta, Goergia. April 11.
Ernest Everett Just, biologist known for research in marine eggs, born. Aug. 14.
Sojourner Truth died in Battle Creek, Michigan. Nov. 26.
George Washington Williams wrote a <u>History of the Negro Race in America</u>, the first serious history undertaken by a Negro.

1884　The Medico-Chirugical Society of the District of Columbia, oldest Black American medical society, organized. April 24.
John Roy Lynch, former Congressman, was elected temporary chairman of the Republican convention, the first Black to preside over deliberations of a national political party. June 3.
Robert Brown Elliott, Reconstructionist, died. Aug. 9.
William Wells Brown died in Cambridge, Massachusetts.

1886　The first electric trolly on the American continent was run by a Black, L. Clark Brooks. May 24.
George Washington Cable published a frank treatment of Negro problems in <u>The Silent South</u>.
William Whipper, underground railroad leader, died.

1888　Slavery in Brazil abolished. May 14.

1889　Provident Hospital was incorporated in Chicago with the first training school for Black nurses. Jan. 23.
Asa Philip Randolph, labor leader, born in Crescent City, Florida. April 15.
Frederick Douglass appointed United States Minister to Haiti.

1891　Peter Jackson, great Black boxer, fought sixty-one round draw with James J. Corbett. May 21.

1892　Luther P. Jackson, Black historian, born in Lexington, Kentucky. July 11.
Lynchings in the United States reached their peak.

1893　Walter Francis White, long-time Executive Secretary of the NAACP, born in Atlanta, Georgia. July 1.
Dr. Daniel Hale Williams performed the world's first successful heart operation at Chicago's Provident Hospital. July 9.

1895   Frederick Douglass died in Anacosta Heights, District of Columbia, where his home is now a national shrine. Feb. 20.
Booker T. Washington delivered his famous "Atlanta Compromise" address at Cotton Exposition in Atlanta, Georgia. Sept. 18.
William Grant Still, orchestral musician and composer ("Afro-American Symphony") born. May 11.
Charles E. Houston, considered one of the great constitutional lawyers in American history, born.
W. E. B. Du Bois received his doctorate degree from Harvard University, the first Black to receive this degree from Harvard. June.
Ida B. Well compiled the first statistical pamphlet on lynching, The Red Record.

1896   United States Supreme Court decision of Plessy v. Ferguson upheld doctrine of "separate but equal." May 18.
National Association of Colored Women organized in Washington, D.C. by Dr. Mary Church Terrell. July 21.
W. E. B. Du Bois' The Suppression of the African Slave Trade was published as the first volume in the Harvard Historical Studies Series.
Booker T. Washington received the first honorary degree awarded to a Black by Harvard University.

1897   H. A. Rucker served as Collector of Internal Revenue in Georgia. Nov. 4.
John Mercer Langston of Virginia, soldier, educator, Haitian consul, Congressman, died. Nov. 15.

1898   Blanche K. Bruce died in Washington, D.C. March 17.
Bob Cole's A Trip to Coontown was the first musical comedy written by a Black for Black talent.
The North Carolina Mutual Life Insurance Company was organized by John Merrick and Dr. A. M. Moore in Durham, North Carolina.

1899   Edward Kennedy ("Duke") Ellington born in Washington, D.C. April 4.

1900   Louis Armstrong born in New Orleans. July 4.
James Augustine Healy died in Portland, Maine. Aug. 5.
Charles W. Chestnutt published his first novel, The House Behind the Cedars.

CHRONOLOGY

1901   Hiram R. Revels died in Holy Springs, Mississippi. Jan. 16.
William M. Trotter founded the Boston Guardian, a militant newspaper which advocated absolute equality for Blacks.

1903   Countee Cullen, distinguished Black poet of the twenties, born. May 30.
W. E. B. Du Bois published his Souls of Black Folk.

1904   Dr. Charles R. Drew, "Father of Blood Plasma," born. June 3.
Dr. Ralph J. Bunche born in Washington, D.C. Aug. 7.

1905   Group of Black intellectuals organized the so-called Niagra Movement at a meeting near Niagra Falls. July 11-13.
Robert S. Abbott began publication of the Chicago Defender, the most influential and militant Black newspaper.

1906   Paul Laurence Dunbar the poet died in Dayton, Ohio. Feb. 9.
The Atlanta race riot resulted in the death of twelve people. Sept. 22.
Alpha Phi Alpha, the first Black Greek letter society was organized as a fraternity. Dec. 4.

1907   Alaine L. Locke of Harvard was the first Black American Rhodes Scholar.
Jack Johnson defeated Tommy Burns for the heavy-weight championship at Sydney, Australia.

1908   Thurgood Marshall born in Baltimore, Maryland. Nov. 29.

1909   NAACP founded on Lincoln's birthday after a savage Springfield, Illinois, lynching. Feb. 12.
Commander Robert E. Perry reached the North Pole accompanied by his "Negro assistant," Matthew H. Henson. April 6.
Miss Caroline Phelp-Stokes of New York, who created a fund for the education of Blacks, died.
Nannie Burroughs founded the National Training School for Women at Washington, D.C.

1910   W. E. B. Du Bois started Crisis as the official organ of the NAACP.
National Urban League organized in New York City. April.

1912   W. C. Handy published the first blues composition, Memphis Blues. Sept. 27.

1913   Harriet Tubman died in Auburn, New York. March 10.

1914   Joe Louis (Barrow) born in Lexington, Alabama. May 13.
The Spingarn Medal awards were instituted by Joel E. Spingarn, Chairman of the Board of Directors of the NAACP, to call to the attention of the American people the existence of distinguished merit and achievement among colored Americans.

1915   Professor Ernest E. Just received the first Spingarn Medal for researches in the field of biology. Feb. 12.
Guinn v. United States declared "grandfather clauses" in the Maryland and Oklahoma constitutions null and void. June 21.
Association of the Study of Negro Life and History founded by Dr. Carter G. Woodson. Sept. 9.
Booker T. Washington died in Tuskegee, Alabama. Nov. 14.
Private Stephen Little, Co. O. 12th Infantry, killed in action, Nogales, Arizona; military camp named in his honor. Nov. 26.
Dr. Robert Russa Moton elected principal, Tuskegee Normal and Industrial Institute. Dec. 20.
About 2,000,000 Southern Blacks moved to Northern industrial centers after the "great migration" began in this year.

1916   Major Charles Young received Spingarn Medal for services in Liberia. Feb. 22.

1917   United States entered World War I.
Harry T. Burleigh, composer, pianist, singer, awarded Spingarn Medal for excellence in the field of creative music. May 16.
Julius Rosenwald Fund for Education, Scientific and Religious Purposes was organized. Oct. 30.
Six hundred Blacks were commissioned officers during World War I.
Edward A. Johnson first Black to be elected to the New York State Assembly. Nov. 23.
Emmett J. Scott was appointed special assistant to the Secretary of War.

1918   William Stanley Braithwaite, poet, literary critic and editor, received Spingarn medal for distinguished achievement in literature. May 5.
National Liberty Congress of Colored Americans petitioned Congress to make lynching a federal crime. July 29.

First soldiers in American army to be decorated for bravery in France were two Blacks, Henry Johnson and Needham R Roberts.

1919   First Pan African Congress, organized by W. E. B. Du Bois, met at Grand Hotel in Paris. Feb. 19-21.
Archibald K. Grimke, former U.S. Consul in Santo Domingo, author and president of the NAACP branch in the District of Columbia for seventy years, received the Spingarn Medal for distinguished service to his race and country. June 27.
There were eighty-three lynchings, the KKK held more than two hundred public meetings across the country, and there were twenty-five major race riots in the country this year.

1920   W. E. B. Du Bois awarded Spingarn Medal for his achievements in scholarship, as editor of Crisis, and for founding and calling of the Pan African Congress. June 1.
National Convention of Marcus Garvey's Universal Improvement Association opened in Liberty Hall in Harlem; Garvey's black nationalist movement reached its peak during this year. Aug. 1.
Emperor Jones, by O'Neill, opened at the Provincetown Theatre starring Charles Gilpin in the title role. Nov. 3.

1921   Charles S. Gilpin, actor, received the Spingarn Medal for his performance in the title role of Eugene O'Neill's drama, Emperor Jones. June 30.
Marcus Garvey inaugurated provisional president of the "Republic of Africa." Aug. 31.
The doctor of philosophy degree was awarded for the first time to Black women: Evan B. Dykes, English at Radcliffe; Sadie T. Mossell, Economics at the University of Pennsylvania; Georgiana R. Simpson, German at the University of Chicago.

1922   Colonel Charles Young died in Liberia. Jan. 7.
Congress passed the Dyer Anti-Lynching Bill. Jan. 26.
Mary B. Talbert, former president of the National Association of Colored Women, awarded Spingarn Medal for service to the women of her race and the restoration of the Frederick Douglass home. June 20.
Frederick Douglass Memorial Home in Washington, D.C. dedicated as museum. Aug. 12.

1923   Spingarn Medal awarded to George Washington Carver, head of the Department of Research, and director of the

Experiment Station at Tuskegee Institute, Alabama, for distinguished research in agricultural chemistry. Sept. 4.
First Catholic seminary for the education of Black priests was dedicated in Bay St. Louis, Mississippi. Sept. 16.
United States Department of Labor estimated that almost 500,000 Blacks left the South during the previous twelve months. Oct. 24.
Charles S. Johnson began to edit <u>Opportunity: A Journal of Negro Life</u> for the Urban League.

1924   Roland Hayes, singer, given Spingarn Medal for his great artistry through which he "so finely interpreted the beauty and charm of the Negro folk song" and won for himself a place as soloist with the Boston Symphony Orchestra. July 1.
Fletcher Henderson, first musician to make name with jazz band, opened at Roseland Ballroom on Broadway. Oct. 3.

1925   Charles Drew of Washington, D.C. won Amherst College Ashley Grid Trophy for being most valuable member of the 1924 squad. Jan. 1.
Adelbert H. Roberts elected to Illinois state legislature--first Negro since reconstruction days. Jan. 10.
Greewood, Mississippi, ministers and prominent businessmen led mob which lynched two Blacks. March 14.
Countee P. Cullen, New York University poet, awarded honorary Phi Beta Kappa key. March 28.
Mob at Oscella, Louisiana, flogged and shot minister for "preaching equality." April 18.
A. Philip Randolph organized Brotherhood of Sleeping Car Porters, a labor union. May 8.
Harry T. Burleigh honored by Temple Emmanuel Congregation of New York City at end of 25th year as soloist. May 16.
James Weldon Johnson, former U.S. consul in Venezuela and Nicaragua, former editor, secretary, NAACP, poet received Spingarn Medal for distinguished achievements as author, diplomat and public servant. June 30.
Louis Armstrong recorded first of "Hot Five and Hot Seven" recordings which influenced jazz. Nov. 11.

1926   Spingarn Medal to Carter G. Woodson, historian and founder of the Association for the Study of Negro Life and History, for ten years' devoted service in collecting and publishing the records of the Black in America. June 29.
Dr. William S. Scarborough, scholar and educator, died. Aug. 9.

CHRONOLOGY

1927 — United States Supreme Court struck down law in Texas barring Blacks from voting "white primary." March 7.
Anthony Overton, businessman, given Spingarn Medal for his successful business career climaxed by the admission of his company as the first Black organization permitted to do insurance business under the rigid requirements of the State of New York. June 28.

1928 — Charles W. Chestnutt, author, awarded Spingarn Medal for his "pioneer work as a literary artist depicting the life and struggle of Americans of Negro descent, and for his long and useful career as scholar, worker and freeman in one of America's greatest cities." July 3.
Oscar de Priest was the first Black from non-Southern state to be elected to Congress. Nov. 6.

1929 — Martin Luther King, Jr. born in Atlanta, Georgia. Jan. 15.
Brotherhood of Sleeping Car Porters received charter from AFL. Feb. 23.
Mordecai Wyatt Johnson, president of Howard University, received Spingarn Medal "for his successful administration as first Black president of the leading Black university in America, and especially for his leadership in securing, during the past year, legal authority for appropriations to Howard University by the government of the United States." July 2.
W. T. Francis, appointed American consul to Liberia by President Coolidge, died in Africa. July 15.
There were ten known lynchings in the United States during the year; Florida led with four.
Francis E. Rivers first Black admitted to the New York Bar Association.

1930 — Green Pastures opened on Broadway featuring Richard B. Harrison as "De Lawd." Feb. 26.
Spingarn Medal to Henry A. Hunt, principal for Fort Valley High and Industrial School "for twenty-five years of modest, faithful, unselfish and devoted service in the education of colored people of rural Georgia and the teaching profession in that state." May 3.
The New York Times announced that the "n" in "Negro" would hereafter be capitalized. June 7.
Mrs. Mary McLeod Bethune was selected as one of the fifty leading women of America compiled by contemporary social historian Ida Tarbell. June 22.
Joel E. Spingarn elected President of NAACP.

Charles Gilpin, noted actor, died.
Jack Thompson became welterweight champion of the world when he defeated Jackie Fields. May 9.

1931 Richard B. Harrison received Spingarn Medal for his "fine and reverent characterization of the Lord in Marc Connelly's play, The Green Pastures (which) has made that play the outstanding dramatic accomplishment in the year 1931. But the Medal is given to Mr. Harrison not simply for this crowning accomplishment, but for the long years of his work as dramatic reader and entertainer, interpreting to the mass of colored people in church and school the finest specimens of English drama from Shakespeare down. It is fitting that in the sixty-seventh year of his life he should receive widespread acclaim for a role that typifies and completes his life work." March 22.
The cause celebre trial of the decade, the Scottsboro trial, began in Alabama. April 6.
Dr. Daniel Hale Williams, founder of Chicago's Provident Hospital, died. Aug. 4.

1932 Spingarn Medal to Robert Russa Moton, principal of Tuskegee Institute, "for his thoughtful leadership of conservative opinion and action on the Negro in the United States, as shown in the U.S. Veterans' Hospital controversy at Tuskegee; by his stand on education in Haiti; by his support of equal opportunity for the Negro in the American public school system; and by his expression of the best ideals of the Negro in his book, What the Negro Thinks." May 20.

1933 NAACP made its first attack on segregation and discrimination in education and filed suit against the University of North Carolina on behalf of Thomas Hocutt; case was lost on technicality. March 15.
Max Yergan, for ten years American Y.M.C.A. secretary among the native students of South Africa, received the Spingarn Medal as "a missionary of intelligence, tact and self-sacrifice, representing the gift of cooperation and culture which American Negroes may send back to their Motherland; and he inaugurated last year an unusual local movement for interracial understanding among black and white students." July 1.

1934 Mississippi Senate passed a law permitting a private citizen, one C. W. Collins, to spring the trap to hang three Blacks accused of raping Collins' daughter. March 10.

CHRONOLOGY

Spingarn Medal to William Taylor Buwell Williams, dean of Tuskegee Institute, "for his long service as field agent of the Slater and Jeanes Funds and the General Education Board, his comprehensive knowledge of the field of Negro education and educational equipment, and his sincere efforts for their betterment." June 29.
Arthur Mitchell defeated Oscar de Priest for the Illinois Congressional seat held by the latter. Nov. 7.
Dr. W. E. B. Du Bois resigned as editor of the <u>Crisis</u>.
Bishop W. Sampson Brooks, founder of Monrovia College in Liberia, died in San Antonio, Texas.

1935
Richard B. Harrison died in New York City. March 18.
Joe Louis defeated Primo Carnera at Yankee Stadium. June 25.
Spingarn Medal to Mrs. Mary McLeod Bethune, founder and president of Bethune Cookman College, Daytona Beach, Florida. "In the face of almost insuperable difficulties she has, almost single-handedly, established and built up Bethune-Cookman College . . . In doing this she has not simply created another educational institution. Both the institution's and Mrs. Bethune's influence have been nationwide. That influence has always been on a high plane, directed by a superb courage. Mrs. Bethune has always spoken out against injustice, in the South as well as in the North, without compromise or fear." June 28.
Maryland Court of Appeals ordered University of Maryland to admit Donald Mung. Nov. 5.
National Council of Negro Women founded in New York City with Mrs. Mary McLeod Bethune as president. Dec. 5.

1936
John Hope, president of Atlanta University, winner of the Spingarn Medal. Characterized by the Committee of Award as "a distinguished leader of his race, one of the foremost college presidents in the United States, widely and favorably known throughout the educational world." July 3.
Jesse Owens won four gold medals at the Berlin Olympics. Aug. 9.
NAACP filed first suits in campaign to equalize teachers' salaries and educational facilities. Dec. 8.

1937
William H. Hastie confirmed as judge of Federal District Court in Virgin Islands, thereby becoming the first Black federal judge. March 26.
Joe Louis defeated James J. Braddock in Chicago for the heavyweight boxing championship of the world. June 22.

Walter White, executive secretary of the NAACP, won the Spingarn Medal for his personal investigation of 41 lynchings and 8 race riots and for his "remarkable tact, skill and persuasiveness" in lobbying for a federal anti-lynching bill. July 2.
Death of Bessie Smith in Clarksdale, Mississippi. Sept. 26.
Bishop Isaac Lane died at the age of 103.

1938

James Weldon Johnson died. June 24.
First woman Black legislator, Crystal Bird Fauset of Philadelphia, elected to the Pennsylvania House of Representatives. Nov. 8.
United States Supreme Court ruled that states must provide equal educational facilities within its boundaries. Dec. 12.
No Spingarn Medal awarded this year.

1939

Broadway opening of <u>Mamba's Daughter</u> gave Ethel Waters her greatest stage triumph. Jan. 14.
D. E. Howard received a patent for his invention of "an optical apparatus for indicating the position of a tool." Jan. 24.
University of Wisconsin refused gift whose donor limited use of funds to white students only. Feb. 18.
Mrs. Franklin D. Roosevelt resigned from the organization of Daughters of Revolution when Marian Anderson was barred from singing in Constitution Hall in Washington, D.C. March.
Marian Anderson gave her Easter Sunday Open Air recital in Washington, D.C.
NAACP launched drive to obtain one million signatures on anti-lynch petition. April 22.
Mississippi Senator Theodore C. Bilbo introduced "Back to Africa Bill" in the United States Senate. April 23.
Joe Louis knocked out Tony Galento in the 4th round. June 28.
Spingarn Medal to Marian Anderson, contralto, ". . . has been chosen for her special achievement in the field of music. Equally with that achievement, which has won her world-wide fame as one of the greatest singers of our time, is her magnificent dignity as a human being. Her unassuming manner, which has not been changed by her phenomenal success, has added to the esteem not only of Marian Anderson as an individual but of the race to which she belongs." July 2.
J. Matilda Bolin appointed first Black woman judge in the United States; she was made judge of the Court of Domestic Relations in New York City by Mayor Fiorello La Guardia. July 22.

CHRONOLOGY 33

NAACP Legal Defense and Educational Fund organized as separate organization. Oct. 11.

1940 Richard Wright's Native Son was published and became one of of the best-sellers of the year. Feb.
Virginia legislature chose "Carry Me Back to Ole Virginia" by Black composer James A. Bland as the state song. April.
Marcus Garvey died in London. June 10.
Louis T. Wright, surgeon, awarded Spingarn Medal "for his contributions to the healing of mankind and for his courageous, uncompromising position held often in the face of bitter attack, that Negro men of medicine should measure up to the most absolute standards of technical excellence and, as a corollary, that havind done so, Negro medical mena and nurses should be accorded every opportunity to serve, without discrimination on account of race or color." July 19.
Benjamin Oliver Davis, Sr. was appointed Brigadier General, the first Black general in the history of the American armed forces. Oct. 16.

1941 George Washington Carver awarded the honorary Doctor of Science degree at the University of Rochester. June 18.
United States Supreme Court ruled in railroad Jim Crow case brought by Congressman Arthur Mitchell that separate facilities must be substantially equal. April 28.
Richard Wright, author, received Spingarn Medal because "he has given to Americans who have eyes to see a picture which must be faced if democracy is to survive . . . For his powerful depiction in his books, Uncle Tom's Children and Native Son, of the effect of proscription, segregation and denial of opportunities on the American Negro." June 27.
President Franklin D. Roosevelt established a Fair Employment Practices Commission. July 19.
Dorie Miller of Waco, Texas, messman on USS "Arizona," manned machine gun during Pearl Harbor attack and downed four enemy planes; later awarded Navy Cross. Dec. 7.

1942 Group of Negro and white men and women committed to direct non-violent action organized the Congress of Racial Equality in Chicago. June.
Bernard W. Robinson, Harvard Medical student, made an ensign in the United States Naval Reserve and was first Black to win a Commission in the United States Navy. June 18.
Spingarn Medal to A. Phillip Randolph, labor leader, international president of the Brotherhood of Sleeping Car Porters,

"for his unparalleled record of leadership in the field of labor organization and national affairs for a period of more than three decades . . . in recognition of the dramatic culmination of his years of effort in the mobilization of Negro mass opinion in 1941 in a March on Washington to exercise the constitutional right of citizens of a democracy to petition their government peaceably for the redress of grievances/ which/ was instrumental in securing the issuance on June 25, 1941, by the President of the United States of an executive order banning discrimination on account of race, creed, color, or national origin in defense industries and in the federal government, and creating the Committee on Fair Employment Practices to effectuate the order." July 19.
William L. Dawson elected to Congress from Chicago. Nov. 3.

1943
Death of George Washington Carver in Tuskegee, Alabama. Jan. 5.
George Gerswin's Porgy and Bess opened on Broadway starring Anne Brown and Todd Duncan. Feb. 28.
Booker T. Washington was the first American merchant ship commanded by a Black captain, High Malzoc, launched at Wilmington, Delaware.
William H. Hastie, jurist and educator, awarded Spingarn Medal "for his distinguished career as a jurist and as an uncompromising champion of equal justice. His every act, and particularly his protest against racial bigotry in an army fighting for the democratic processes, has established a standard of character and conduct." June 6.
Race riot in Detroit. Thirty-four killed; federal troops called out. June 16.
Major race riot broke out in Harlem. Aug. 1-2.
Lt. Charles Hall, Brazil, Indiana, was first American Black to shoot down Nazi plane. July 2.

1944
United States Supreme Court in Smith v. Allwright, banned the "white primary" which had effectively prevented Blacks in the South from voting. April 24.
United Negro College Fund established. April 24.
Dr. Mary E. Branch, president of Tillotson College, Austin, Texas, died. July 8.
Spingarn Medal awarded to Dr. Charles R. Drew, scientist, "for his outstanding work in blood plasma. Dr. Drew's research in this field led to the establishment of a blood plasma bank which served as one of the models for the widespread system of blood banks used by the American

Red Cross. Dr. Drew was appointed full-time Medical Director for the blood plasma project for Great Britain. The report on this work was published and served as a guide for later developments for the United States Army and for the armies of our Allies." July 16.
Death of composer Will Marion Cook. July 20.
Black historian Edward A. Johnson died. July 24.
Adam Clayton Powell elected first Black Congressman from the East. Aug. 1.
Anna Lucasta, starring Hilda Simms and Frederick O'Neil, opened on Broadway and was one of the year's great stage successes. Aug. 20.
SS Frederick Douglass, first ship named for a Black, was sunk by enemy action. Aug. 20.
Black servicewomen sworn into WAVES for first time. Dec. 13.

1945
First state Fair employment Practices Commission was established in New York State. March 12.
One thousand white students walked out of Gary, Indiana, schools to protest school integration. Sept. 18.
Paul Robeson, singer and actor, received Spingarn Medal for "distinguished achievement in the theatre and on the concert stage." Oct. 18.
Irving C. Molleson, Chicago Republican, sworn in as United States Customs Judge. Nov. 3.
More than one million Blacks were inducted or drafted into the United States armed forces by the time World War II ended.

1946
Countee Cullen, poet, died in New York City. Jan. 9.
William H. Hastie confirmed as governor of the Virgin Islands. May 1.
Mrs. E. C. Clement first Black named "Mother of the Year." May 1.
Supreme Court banned segregation in interstate bus travel. June 3.
Thurgood Marshall, special counsel of the NAACP, given Spingarn Medal for "his distinguished service as a lawyer before the Supreme Court of the United States and inferior courts, particularly in the Texas Primary Case, which conceivably may have more far-reaching influence than any other act in the ending of disfranchisement based upon race or color in the country." June 28.

1947	Jackie Robinson joined the Brooklyn Dodgers, first Black in organized baseball in modern times. April 10.
Dr. Percy L. Julian, research chemist, received the Spingarn Medal "in recognition of his work as a distinguished chemist who has made many important discoveries that have saved many lives. He has demonstrated technical skill, courage and sustained effort on the highest level in making contributions that will benefit mankind for years to come." June 27.
President's Committee on Civil Rights condemned racial injustices in America in a formal report, "To Secure These Rights." Oct. 29.
1948	First Lt. Nancy C. Leftenant was first Black accepted in the regular Army Nurse Corps. Feb. 12.
United States Supreme Court declared restrictive housing covenants unenforceable in the courts (Shelly. v. Kraemer) May 3.
Black elected for the first time to the American Nurses' Association Board of Directors. June 12.
A. Philip Randolph formed the League for Non-Violent Civil Disobedience Against Military Segregation. June 26.
Spingarn Medal awarded to Channing H. Tobias, "in recognition of his consistent role as a defender of fundamental American liberties . . . He brought to the President's Committee on Civil Rights intellectual vitality, courage and the richness of his long experience in the field of race relations. Largely due to his persistence and clear insight the committee produced a report of historic significance in man's unending struggle for justice." June 27.
Poet Claude McKay died in Chicago.
1949	Congressman William L. Dawson became Chairman of House Expenditures Committee, the first Black to head a standing Committee in Congress. Jan. 18.
Palisades, New Jersey, swimming pool integrated after two-year non-violent campaign. June 1.
Wesley A. Brown was first Black to graduate from Annapolis Naval Academy. June 3.
United States Navy Department announced policy of equality of treatment and opportunity to all persons in Navy and Marine Corps. June 7.
Dr. Ralph J. Bunche, international civil servant, awarded Spingarn Medal "for his distinguished scholarship in the Myrdal study, his painstaking efforts as director of the United Nations Trusteeship Division, but principally for

his priceless contribution to the settlement of armed conflict in the Middle East." June 17.
Station W E R D was opened as the first Black owned radio station in the United States in Atlanta, Georgia. Oct. 3.
William H. Hastie nominated for United States Circuit Court of Appeals. Oct. 15.
Famed dancer Bill Robinson of stage and screen died in New York City. Nov.25.

1950 James Weldon Johnson Memorial Collection of Black Arts and Letters given to Yale University by Charles Van Vechten. Jan. 8.
Dr. Charles R. Drew, pioneer in blood research, died. April 1.
Death of Dr. Carter G. Woodson in Washington, D.C. April 3.
Attorney-General MacGrath and Solicitor-General Perlman argued before the U.S. Supreme Court for the reversal of 1896 ruling which upheld segregation. April 4.
Charles H. Houston, leading constitutional lawyer, died. April 22.
While holding against segregation in the three cases before it, the U.S. Supreme Court avoided general ruling on "separate but equal" doctrine. June 6.
Spingarn Medal awarded posthumously to Charles H. Houston, Chairman, NAACP Legal Committee and "stalwart defender of democracy, inspired teacher of youth, and leader in the legal profession . . . in memory of a lifetime of gallant championship of equal rights for all Americans, of unselfish devotion to democratic ideals, of unswerving fidelity to the American dream of equal opportunity." June 25.
American Medical Association seated first Black delegate. June 26.
Mrs. E. Sampson was first United States Black appointed as representative to the United Nations. Aug. 19.
Dr. Ralph J. Bunche was the first American Black to receive the Nobel Peace Prize. Sept. 22.
Althea Gibson filed entry for national tennis championship; first Negro accepted. Oct. 26.

1951 National Association of Colored Graduate Nurses disbanded since aim to integrate Blacks into nursing profession achieved. Jan. 27.
University of North Carolina admitted first Black student in its history. April 24.

Oscar De Priest, former Congressman from Illinois, died. May 12.
Dr. Ralph J. Bunche first Black to win honorary degree from Princeton, New Jersey. June 13.
Spingarn Award to Mabel Keaton Staupers, who, as a leader of the National Association of Colored Nurses, "spearheaded the successful movement to integrate Black nurses into American life as equals," and whose work was "characterized by wisdom, vision, courage and refusal to equivocate," as a result of which the NACGN was dissolved as no longer needed. June 29.
Carver National Monument in Joplin, Missouri dedicated; first national park honoring Blacks. July 14.
Harry T. Moore, NAACP Coordinator for Florida, killed by bomb blast in house. Dect. 27.
Pfc. W. H. Thompson given Medal of Honor posthumously for Korean War action; first Black to receive this since Spanish-American War.
Riots in Cicero, Illinois, worst since 1919.
Martin Luther King, Jr. received the Bachelor of Divinity degree from Crozier Theological Seminary, Chester, Pennsylvania.

1952   University of Tennessee admitted its first Black student. Jan. 12.
Judge Waring quit his Charleston, South Carolina home as a result of ostracism for his fight for Blacks. Feb. 24.
Spingarn Medal awarded posthumously to Harry T. Moore, NAACP leader in the State of Florida, and a martyr in the "crusade for freedom," for "his invaluable contributions and his courage in working for full implementation of the democratic ideal," including justice in the courts, the abolition of segregation at the University of Florida, and the expansion of the Black vote in the state. Assassinated by a hate bomb in his home at Mims on Christmas night, 1951. June 27.
Ford Theatre of Baltimore dropped segregation policy in effect since 1861.
Southern Regional Council reported forty bombings since January 1951. Dec. 7.
Tuskegee Institute reported that 1952 was the first year in seventy-one years of tabulation that there were no reported lynchings. Dec. 30.

1953   Fisk was first Black institution of higher education in United States to get Phi Beta Kappa chapter. April 5.

United States Supreme Court ruled that District of Columbia restaurants could not legally refuse to serve Blacks. June 8.
Albert W. Dent of Dillard University was elected President of the National Health Council. June 20.
NAACP set integregation as goal, dropped "separate but equal" theory. June 23.
Paul R Williams, distinguished architect, awarded Spingarn Medal for his pioneer contributions as a creative designer of livable and attractive modern dwellings and beautiful utilitarian commercial structures--contributions which have won for him the respect and admiration of his fellow architects and high rank in his chosen profession. June 26.
Drama by Black playwright Louis Peterson, Take a Giant Step, opened on Broadway. Sept. 24.
Hulan Jack elected president of the Borough of Manhattan. Nov. 4.

1954

J. Ernest Wilkins of Chicago appointed Assistant Secretary of Labor by President Dwight Eisenhower, April 23.
Landmark United States Supreme Court case, Brown v. Board of Education, et al. declared that racial segregation in public schools was unconstituional. May 17.
White Brotherhood set up in Georgia to retain segregation. June 6.
E. L. Ashford of Pacific Coast League was first Black umpire in organized baseball. June 13.
Spingarn Medal to Theodore K. Lawless, physician, educator, and philanthropist, recognized as one of the world's leading dermatologists, for his extensive research and experiments which have enlarged the area of scientific knowledge in his chosen field. July 4.
First White Citizens Council unit was organized in Indianola, Mississippi. July 11.
Charles V. Bush was first Black page boy in Supreme Court and first in Capitol page school. July 24.
Mary Church Terrell died in Washington, D.C. July 24.
Dr. F. M. Snowden appointed cultural attache in embassy in Rome; first Black in major embassy post. Aug. 19.
S. Richardson named Chairman of the Federal Parole Board; first Black on Board. Sept. 29.
Benjamin Davis, Jr. appointed first Black general in the Air Force. Oct. 27.
Defense Department announced all units in the armed forces were now integrated. Oct. 30.
Carol Williams engaged by Sadler Wells Opera. Nov. 26.
Track star M. Whitman first Black to win Sullivan Tropy, top United States amateur award. Dec. 31.

1955 Marian Anderson made her debut at the Metropolitan Opera House; she was the first Black singer in the company's history. Jan. 7.
Charlie Parker, one of the founders of the modern jazz movement, died. March 12.
Death of Walter White, NAACP leader, in New York City. March 21.
Roy Wilkins appointed Executive Secretary of NAACP. April 11.
Mrs. Mary McLeod Bethune died in Daytona Beach, Florida. May 18.
U.S. Supreme Court decree for the implementation of the May 17, 1954, school desegregation decision; "with all due and deliberate speed." May 31.
Spingarn Medal awarded to Carl Murphy, dedicated editor, publisher and far-sighted civic leader, for his leadership role in leveling invidious racial barriers in employment, education and recreation. June 26.
E. F. Morrow appointed administrative officer in the Eisenhower Executive Office. July 8.
Georgia Education Board ordered lifetime ban on teachers who instructed "mixed" classes. July 11.
Emmet Till, fourteen years old, was kidnapped and lynched in Money, Mississippi. Aug. 28.
Interstate Commerce Commission banned segregation in buses, waiting rooms and travel coaches involved in interstate travel. Nov. 25.
Bus boycott initiated in Montgomery, Alabama. Dec. 5.

1956 Autherine Lucy admitted to University of Alabama. Feb. 3.
National Press Club admitted L. R. Lautier as first Black. Feb. 5.
Miss Lucy suspended after riot at University of Alabama. Feb. 7.
Manifest denouncing U.S. Supreme Court ruling on segregation in public schools was issued by one hundred Southern Senators and Representatives. March 11-12.
U.S. Supreme Court banned segregation in public parks, playgrounds, beaches and golf courses; rejected "separate but equal" doctrine.
Leontyne Price was first Black to sing before mixed audience in Laurel, Mississippi.
Louisville, Kentucky, schools integrated. Sept. 10.
Dr. John Hope Franklin appointed chairman of the history department at Brooklyn College.
Jack ("Jackie") R. Robinson, brilliant and versatile athlete,

received Spingarn Medal for "his superb sportsmanship, his pioneer role in opening up a new field of endeavor for young Blacks, and his civic consciousness." Dec. 8.

1957　Martin Luther King, Jr. elected president of Southern Christian Leadership Conference at its organization meeting in New Orleans. Jan. 12.
Robert Ming, Chicago lawyer, elected Chairman of American Veterans Committee, first Black to head major national veterans organization. April 28.
Spingarn Medal awarded to Martin Luther King, Jr., dedicated and selfless clergyman, for his creative contributions to the Fight for Freedom and his outstanding leadership role in the successful Montgomery bus protest movement. June 28.
Althea Gibson won women's Single Championship at Wimbledom, England and the United States Law Tennis Championship. July 7, 22.
Booker T. Washington National Monument opened at Rocky Mount, Virginia; second such memorial to a Black leader. July 28.
Rev. A. J. Carey, Jr. appointed Chairman of President's Government Employment Policy Committee; first Black in this position. Aug. 6.
Prayer Pilgrimage, the largest civil rights demonstration staged by American Blacks up to that time, held in Washington, D.C.
Congress passed the first Civil Rights Act since 1875. Aug. 29.
President Eisenhower ordered federal troops to Little Rock, Arkansas, to prevent interference with school integration at Central High School. Sept. 24.
New York City was first to legislate against racial or religious discrimination in housing with the adoption of its Fair Housing Practice law. Dec. 5.

1958　Clifton R. Wharton confirmed as Minister to Rumania. Feb. 5.
Mrs. Daisy Bates and the Little Rock Nine awarded Spingarn Medal for "their pioneer role in upholding the basic ideal of American democracy in the face of continuing harassment and constant threats of bodily injury." July 11.
Members of NAACP Youth Council began series of sit-ins at Oklahoma City lunch counters. Aug. 19.

1959 — First play written by a Black woman, Raisin in the Sun, by Lorraine Hansberry, was one of the major Broadway hits. March 11.
Second "Youth March for Integrated Schools" drew 30,000 students to Washington, D.C. April 18.
Mack Parker lynched in Poplarville, Mississippi. April 25.
Prince Edward County, Virginia, Board of Supervisors abandoned public school system in attempt to prevent school segregation. June 26.
Rev. Dr. King and others urged President Eisenhower to make statement against segregation. July 5.
Billie Holiday, leading blues singer, died in New York City. July 17.
Dade County, Florida, first to desegregate public schools in Florida.
Spingarn Medal given to Edward Kennedy (Duke) Ellington, composer and orchestra leader, for his outstanding musical achievements which have won for him "not only universal acclaim but also worldwide recognition of our country's contribution to the field of music." Sept. 11.
Citizens of Deerfield, Illinois, authorized plan which blocked building of interracial housing development. Dec. 21.

1960 — Forty-three arrested in Raleigh, North Carolina, sit-in. Feb. 10.
Fifty-nine arrested in Chatanooga, Tennessee, sit-in. Feb. 19.
Pope John elevated Bishop Laurian Rugambwa of Tanganyika to College of Cardinals, first Black Cardinal in modern times. March 3.
Students served at Salisbury, North Carolina and at Atlanta, Georgia, lunch counters; students demonstrated in New Orleans. March 7.
Three hundred and fifty protestors arrested and placed in stockade in Orangeburg, South Carolina. March 15.
Forty arrested in sit-ins in four North Carolina cities. March 17.
Thirty-seven Blacks arrested in public libraries in Memphis, Tennessee. March 19.
Twenty-three arrested in art gallery and library in Memphis. March 22.
Lunch counters integrated in Corpus Christi, Texas; sixteen students arrested in Baton Rouge, Louisiana. March 28.
Ten arrested in Birmingham sit-in; White House Conference

on Children and Youth endorsed sit-ins. March 31.
Student Non-Violent Coordinating Committee organized on Shaw University campus. April 15.
Sit-in protest at chain stores in Savannah, Georgia; fifteen arrested picketing chain stores in Ann Arbor, Michigan. April 16.
United States Federal Court ruled that Atlanta, Georgia, must start school segregation by September, 1961. May 9.
Winston-Salem lunch counters integrated. May 25.
Four lunch counters integrated in Oak Ridge, Tennessee, June 4.
Langston Hughes, poet, author and playwright, received Spingarn Medal in recognition of his reputation "in America, Europe, Asia, Africa, Central and South America as a major American writer and considered by many the poet laureate of the Negro race." June 26.
Democratic National Convention adopted Civil Rights plank supporting sit-ins and school integration. July 12.
Elijah Muhammad, black internationalist leader, called for creation of Black state at New York City meeting. July 31.
Southern Regional Council reported that eight cities that desegregated lunch counters maintained "sales as usual."
Southern School News reported that 94% of Blacks in America were attending segregated schools.
During decade of 1950-1960, 1,500,000 Blacks migrated from South to Northern communities.
Richard Wright died in Paris. Nov. 28.

1961 Adam Clayton Powell assumed the Chairmanship of the Education and Labor Committee of the House of Representatives. Jan. 3.
Carl T. Rowan appointed Deputy Assistant Secretary of State for Public Affairs. Jan. 25.
H. Lewis conducted Los Angeles Philharmonic Orchestra; first Black to conduct major symphony orchestra at its home during the regular season. Feb. 10.
Robert Weaver sworn in as Administrator of Housing and Home Finance Agency, highest federal post ever held by an American Black. Feb. 11.
Thirteen "Freedom Riders" began bus trip through the South. May 4.
Soprano Leontyne Price starred in Metropolitan Opera Company's Girl of the Golden West, first Black to open Met season in leading role. May 24.
Marvin Cook named ambassador to Niger Republic; first Black envoy named by Kennedy Administration to African nation. May 26.

C. F. Poole appointed Attorney for Northern California District; first Black in such position appointed in continental United States. April 16.
Jacksonville, Florida, closed its swimming pool to avoid integration. June 13.
Gene Baker, former 2nd baseman for Pittsburgh Pirates, was first Black ex-major leaguer to advance to position of major league farm team. June 20.
Ten "Freedom Riders" sentenced in Tallahasse Airport case. June 23.
George L. P. Weaver named Secretary of Labor in charge of international affairs. July 9.
Spingarn Medal awarded to Kenneth B. Clark, Professor of Psychology at the College of the City of New York; founder and director of the Northside Center for Child Development and prime mobilizer of the resources of modern psychology in the attack upon racial segregation, for his dedicated service and inspired research which contributed significantly to the historic U.S. Supreme Court decision of May 17, 1954, banning segregation in public education. July 16.
President John F. Kennedy nominated Thurgood Marshall to the United States Circuit Court of Appeals. Sept. 23.
Otis Marion Smith became Associate Justice on the Michigan Supreme Court. Oct. 10.
Cincinnati Reds outfielder, Frank Robinson, voted "Most Valuable Player" of the year by Baseball Writers' Association. Nov. 23.
James H. Meredith registered at the University of Mississippi.
United Press International picked Chicago Cubs' outfielder, Billy Williams, as the National League's "Rookie of the Year."
Ernie Davis of Syracuse University was first Black to win Harmon Trophy as college football's "Player of the Year."
American Anthropological Association reaffirmed belief in inherent equality of Blacks and whites. Nov. 21.
Blacks comprised 12% of population in cities of over 1,000,000, compared with 10% of a decade ago. Dec. 3.
In a final blow to "massive resistance," United States courts held unconstitutional a law permitting closing of integration-ordered public school districts.
There was an increase of 17,907 students, or 6% in the South's Black attendance of mixed classes over 1960.
School board presidencies of Oakland, California, and Washington, D.C. went to Blacks, the first Blacks to lead school systems in major United States metropolitan centers.
John Duncan became first Black to serve as Commissioner for Washington, D.C.

Chicago Human Relations Commission reported city's Black population rose from 492,265 to 812,637, in the decade from 1950 to 1960.
1960 Census showed that 1,087,931 Blacks resided in New York City; 14% of city's total population and the largest number of Blacks of any city in the United States.

1962   Jackie Robinson was first Black to be elected to National Baseball Hall of Fame. Jan. 24.
Lt. Commander Samuel L. Gravely given command of destroyer escort, USS Falgout; first Black to command U.S. warship. Jan. 31.
Mattiwilda Dobbs became first person (Negro or white) to sing before integrated audience in Municipal Hall in Atlanta, Georgia. Feb. 1.
John Thomas appointed Director of the Health, Education and Welfare Department's Cuban Refugee Program. March 15.
Census Bureau reported 6,025,173 of 18,871,831 Blacks lived in 25 largest cities; 1,457,000 Blacks migrated from South to northern and western regions in last decade. April 15.
Johnson Publishing Company was first Black company to enter book publishing field. April 25.
Luke C. Moore became first U.S. Marshal since Frederick Douglass held such position. May 9.
John Hope Franklin appointed William Pitt Professor of American History and Institutions at Cambridge University, England, for one year. May 20.
Death of E. Franklin Frazier, noted sociologist and historian, after 45 years of teaching. May 22.
J. O'Neill named Chicago Cubs coach; first Black coach in major leagues. May 30.
W. W. Braithwaite, poet, anthologist and literary critic, died in New York City. June 9.
Big Bill Russell of the Boston Celtics named "Player of the Year" by Sporting News. June 19.
NAACP had more cases before the U.S. Supreme Court than any institution except the federal government. June 18.
Rev. W. E. Houston was first Black elected Moderator of United Presbyterian Church, N.Y. Synod. June 21.
Robert C. Weaver, Administrator, Housing and Home Finance Agency, awarded Spingarn Medal for his long years of dedicated public service at municipal, state and federal levels; for his pioneer role in the development and advocacy of the doctrine of "open occupancy" in housing; and for his responsible and militant leadership in the struggle for human rights. July 8.

Rev. Martin Luther King, Jr. arrested in Albany, Georgia, after anti-segregation demonstration. July 10.

Howard Jenkins, law professor at Howard University, appointed first Black member of the National Labor Relations Board. July 22.

Mel Goode was first Black TV news commentator on network TV (ABC-TV). Aug. 29.

U.S. Supreme Court ruled that University of Mississippi must admit James H. Meredith, a Black Air Force veteran, whose application for admission had been on file for 14 months. Sept. 10.

Hobart Taylor, Jr. appointed Executive Vice-Chairman of the President's Equal Opportunity Committee. Sept. 11.

Mississippi Governor Ross R. Barnett personally denied James H. Meredith admission to University of Mississippi. Sept. 20.

U.S. Circuit Court of Appeals ordered Board of Higher Education of Mississippi to admit Meredith to the University or face contempt charges; Board agreed to comply with order. Sept. 24.

Governor Barnett defied orders of Court and personally interfered with Meredith's attempt to enter the University to register. Sept. 25.

A. Leon Higginbotham nominated as federal judge for eastern Pennsylvania, youngest member of the federal bench in the U.S. Sept. 26.

Thurgood Marshall confirmed as member of Second United States Circuit Court of Appeals after one year delay by Southern opposition in U.S. Senate. Sept. 12.

Four major TV advertisers approved use of Black models in commercials aimed at nation-wide audience.

James Meredith escorted to the campus of the University of Mississippi with Federal Marshals. Sept. 30.

University of Mississippi students and adults from Oxford, Mississippi, and other Southern communities rioted on campus; two killed.

Federal soldiers restored order on campus and in town. Oct. 1.

Accompanied by federal marshals, James Meredith registered at the University. Oct.

Edward W. Brooke elected Attorney General of Massachusetts. Nov. 7.

August Hawkins elected as U.S. Representative from California, first Negro to represent this state. Nov. 7.

Leroy Johnson first Black state legislator elected in Georgia since Reconstruction. Nov. 8.

Gerald Lamb elected Connecticut State Treasurer. Nov. 8.
U.S. Supreme Court ruled that segregation in interstate and intra state travel was unconstitutional.
Diahann Carroll was first black to play romantic lead in an otherwise all-white Broadway musical, Richard Rodgers' No Strings. April 15.
Maury Wills of the Los Angeles Dodgers broke all records in major league baseball as the greatest "baseball thief" (stolen bases).
Wilt Chamberlain of the San Francisco Warriors was first professional basketball player to score 4000 points in a single season.
2000 Blacks were enrolled in previously "whites only" colleges and universities in the South.
There were 948 "token-integrated" public school districts in the all-white southern school districts, an increase of 124 districts over 1961.
Archbishop Joseph F. Rummel directed all Roman Catholic schools in his Louisiana archdiocese to integrate.
Marjorie Lawson became first Black woman judge in Washington, D.C.
Mrs. Ann Roberts appointed FHA Deputy Regional Administrator and became highest ranking Black woman in the federal housing field.
Fourteen Southern airports voluntarily integrated their passenger facilities.
The Albany (Georgia) Movement, comprising the civil rights efforts of several action groups, including CORE, SNCC, SCLC, and the NAACP resulted in the following achievements in social relations: (1) agreement by local authorities to form a bi-racial committee on racial problems; (2) desegregation of the city's bus terminal and cafe; (3) release from jail of movement demonstrators and an end to mass arrests; (4) the substitution of "Mr. & Mrs." for derogatory terms by city officials in addressing Negro citizens.
U.S. Supreme Court authorized Tennessee citizens to sue in federal courts to force reapportionment of legislative districts. This would result in shift of political power from rural segregationist strongholds to the relatively more liberal, heavily Black-populated urban South.

1963

James Baldwin's The Fire Next Time published. Jan. 31
President John F. Kennedy sent his Civil Rights Message to Congress. March 1.
Carl T. Rowan appointed Ambassador to Finland. March 9.
John Thomas appointed Director of the Health, Education,

and Welfare Department's Cuban Refugee Program. March 15.

Dr. John Hope Franklin appointed to the faculty of the University of Chicago. April 14.

Arthur Ashe, 19, was first Black to join the U.S. Davis Cup Tennis Team. May 14.

U.S. Supreme Court ruled that in cities making segregation a matter of public policy, whether by ordinance or executive order, Blacks may not be prosecuted for seeking service in privately owned stores. May 21.

President Kennedy said nation faced "moral crisis" over Black demands for equality; pledged legislation to open public facilities for all (TV address). June 12.

Spingarn Medal awarded to Medgar Wile Evers, NAACP Field Secretary for the State of Mississippi, World War II veteran, hero and martyr felled by an assassin's bullet in the back on June 12; accepted posthumously by his wife. July 4.

Largest civil rights demonstration in history took place at the site of the Lincoln and Washington Memorial in Washington, D.C.; 250,000 persons participated. Aug. 29.

Bomb exploded in Birmingham Negro Baptist Church killing four Black girls; two Black youths killed in racial rioting which followed. Sept. 6.

James W. Silver, Professor of History at the University of Mississippi and retiring President of the Southern Historical Association, charged that Mississippi is "a closed society and a century behind culturally." Nov. 8.

Rev. Benjamin J. Anderson, pastor of Princeton's historic Witherspoon Street Presbyterian Church, was nominated to become the first Black to serve as a moderator of the General Assembly of the United Presbyterian Church. Nov. 30.

Ralph J. Bunche and Marian Anderson were among the recipients of Medals of Freedom from President L. B. Johnson at the White House. Dec. 7.

Dinah Washington died. Dec. 14.

Outfielder Tommy Davis of the Los Angeles Dodgers won baseball's batting crown for the 2nd consecutive year.

William T. Mason Jr. appointed first Black Assistant Federal Attorney in Virginia.

1964

Senator Barry Goldwater called public accommodations section of the Civil Rights Act unconstitutional. Jan. 19.

Carl T. Rowan appointed Director of the United States Information Agency, the highest position ever held by a Black in the federal government. Jan. 21.

Atlanta Constitution, a leading Southern newspaper, reversed a previous position and editorially supported the public accommodations provision of the Civil Rights Act. Jan. 22.
Beckworth trial for murder of Medgar Evers opened. Feb. 1.
A. T. Walden sworn in as Atlanta municipal judge; first Black judge in Georgia since Reconstruction. Feb. 4.
Mistrial in Beckworth trial; jury unable to agree. Feb. 8.
Race riot in Jacksonville, Florida. March 24-26.
U.S. Supreme Court set aside contempt conviction of Black Mary Hamilton who declined to answer in Alabama court when addressed as "Mary." March 31.
Second jury unable to agree in Beckworth case; mistrial declared. April 26.
U. S. Supreme Court ruled that Prince Edward County in Virginia must re-open its public schools on an integrated basis. May 26.
Sidney Poitier won the Academy of Motion Picture Arts and Sciences' Oscar Award as best actor of 1963 for his performance in Lilies of the Field. April.
Three civil rights workers reported missing on Mississippi Sumer Project two weeks after release from jail in Philadelphia, Mississippi. June 23.
Spingarn Medal awarded to Roy Wilkins, Executive Secretary of the NAACP, "despite his own urgent request that this present honor not be conferred upon him," for the "distinctive and immeasurable contribution to the advancement of the American people and the national purpose" in his work on behalf of civil rights movement." June 23.
Race riots in Rochester, New York. July 1.
Civil Rights Act of 1964 passed and signed into law; most far-reaching civil rights legislation since Civil War Amendments. July 3.
Fifteen year old Black James Powell shot and killed by off-duty police Lt. Gilligan in New York City. July 17.
Race riot in Harlem. July 19.
Bodies of civil rights workers Goodman, Schwerner and Chaney found in newly-built earthen dam near Philadelphia, Mississippi. Aug. 5.
Race riots in South Chicago suburb in Dixmoor; 50 hurth. Aug. 17-18.
Philadelphia race riots; 29 hurt. Aug. 29-30.
FBI arrested four Philadelphia, Mississippi, law enforcement officers and former sheriff in connection with murder of three civil rights workers. Oct. 4.
Rev. Martin Luther King, Jr. won Nobel Peace Prize. Oct. 15.

NAACP resumed operations in Alabama for first time since enjoined from operating in state in 1956. Nov. 1.
Negro Baptist Church burned near Ripley, Mississippi. Nov. 1.
Civil Rights struggle in Mississippi has resulted in: three killed, eighty beaten, three wounded by gunfire, over one thousand arrested, thirty-five churches burned, thirty-one homes and other buildings bombed--since the beginning of the year 1964.
Jackson District Attorney announced Beckworth will not be tried for murder of Medgar Evers without new evidence. Nov. 15.
U.S. Supreme Court upheld the constitutionality of the public accommodations section of the Civil Rights Act of 1964. Dec.
Public schools of the District of Columbia were registering a pupil enrollment of 85.7% Black.
Ford Foundation announced grants totalling $15,000,000 to strengthen Black colleges.
Hampton Institute opened its new Communications Center, marking the 125th anniversary of the birth of the founder of Hampton, Samuel C. Armstrong.
Senator Richard B. Russell (Georgia) proposed a voluntary relocation of Blacks proportionately at government expense throughout the states of the federal union.
Arthur B. Spingarn, a founder of NAACP and President since 1940, announced plans to retire at the end of the year.
Erwin S. Perry, who received his Ph. D.. this year from the University of Texas, made such a distinguished record that he was appointed to the University faculty commencing in September.
Hobart Taylor appointed Associate Special Counsel at the White House for President L. B. Johnson, succeeding Theodore C. Sorenson.
National Urban League launched anti-poverty campaign among Blacks under leadership of Whitney Young, Jr.
Clinton E. Knox nominated Ambassador to Dahomey.
John Haynes Holmes, one of founders of NAACP, died.
Three Broadway shows included interracial romances without audience incident: <u>Golden Boy</u>, <u>The Sign in Sidney Brustein's Window</u>, The Owl and the Pussycat.

CHRONOLOGY 51

Black athletes contributed significantly to United States prestige at the XVIII Olympics in Tokyo by winning half of the 36 gold medals awarded American athletes.

1965

Lorraine Vivian Hansberry, leading Black playwright, died in New York City. Jan. 13.

President Lyndon B. Johnson appointed Lisle Carter, a Black, as Assistant Secretary in the Department of Health, Education and Welfare. Jan. 15.

Three men indicted for beating Black civil rights worker in Greenwood, Mississippi, were the first persons to be arrested under the Civil Rights Act of 1964. Jan. 15.

Survey of N. Y. Times of compliance with Civil Rights Act showed substantial compliance with Title II (Public Accommodations) in South, but "painfully slow progress against voting discrimination under Title I." Jan. 16.

Constance Baker Motley, former President of the Borough of Manhattan in New York City, became first Black woman to be appointed to a federal judgeship. Jan. 25.

Governor Edward Breathitt of Kentucky signed Civil Rights law, first of its kind adopted by any state south of the Ohio River. Jan. 25.

Geraldine McCullough was the first Black winner of the Widener Memorial Medal for Sculpture, awarded by the Pennsylvania Academy of Fine Arts. Feb. 3.

United States Civil Rights Commission reported that majority of Southern school districts were evading integration while still adhering to federal guidelines for desegregation. Feb. 15.

Nat "King" Cole, noted singing artist, died in Los Angeles. Feb. 16.

Malcolm X was assassinated in New York City while addressing rally of his followers. Feb. 22.

Wyatt T. Walker, former assistant to Dr. Martin Luther King, Jr., named Special Assistant on Urban Affairs to Governor Nelson Rockefeller of New York. March 1.

Bill Russell of the Boston Celtics was honored as the most valuable player in the National Basketball Association for the fourth time in five years. March 4.

Federal Judge authorized Selma-Montgomery march in Alabama. March 17.

President Lyndon B. Johnson called up 4,000 troops to protect Selma-Montgomery marchers. March 18.

Dr. Martin Luther King, Jr. and Under-Secretary of United Nations Ralph Bunche lead 3,200 on 54 mile Selma-Montgomery march. March 21.

March from Selma ended as 25,000 Blacks and whites rallied in front of capitol, Montgomery, March 25.
Mrs. Crystal Bird Fauset, pioneer female legislator, died. March 30.
The first Black city councilman in the history of San Antonio, Texas, was elected when Rev. S. H. James defeated three candidates. April 8.
St. Thomas Episcopal Church of Philadelphia voted to nullify its 1796 charter restriction that limited membership to "Africans and descendants of African race." April 11.
Soprano Leontyne Price was awarded the Order of Merit of the Italian Republic. April 13.
Bishop Prince A. T. Taylor, Jr. became the first Black to assume the presidency of the Council of Bishops of the Methodist Church. April 23.
J. Raymond Jones elected leader of the powerful New York County Democratic Committee (Tammany Hall). May 22.
Lerone Bennett, Jr., Senior Editor of Ebony Magazine, was awarded the 1965 Patron Saints Award Society of Midland Authors for his biography of Dr. Martin Luther King, Jr., What Manner of Man. June 17.
President Lyndon B. Johnson issued Executive Order creating cabinet-level Council on Equal Opportunity, with Vice-President Humphrey as Chairman, to coordinate civil rights activities of all federal agencies. July 7.
The 1965 Voting Rights Act, providing for the registration by federal examiners of those Black voters turned away by state officials, signed by President Lyndon B. Johnson.

1966

Arthur B. Spingarn retired as President of NAACP after serving since 1940. Jan. 3.
Robert C. Henry unanimously elected mayor of Springfield, Ohio, by City Council, the first Black to become mayor of an Ohio city. Jan. 3.
Floyd B. McKissick appointed National Director of CORE, Jan. 4.
H. B. Perry installed as Auxillary Bishop of New Orleans, first Black to hold that position in the United States since 1875. Jan. 7.
Bertram L. Baker became Assembly Majority Whip in the New York State legislature, first Black to win a leadership position in the state's legislature. Jan. 10.
Robert C. Weaver appointed by President L. B. Johnson as Secretary of Housing and Urban Development, first Black to serve in a President's Cabinet. Jan. 14.

CHRONOLOGY

The United Negro College Fund received a grant of $2,000,000 from United States Steel Corporation.

Andrew Brimmer appointed to the Federal Reserve Banking Board, first Black to serve on the Board. Feb. 27.

Announcement was made that the new Smithsonian Institute in Washington, D.C., will hand in the Hall of Historic Americans in the Museum of History and Technology exhibits illustrating the progress of the civil rights movement from the earliest slave days to the March on Washington in 1963.

United States Supreme court upheld major provisions of 1965 Voting Rights Act, rejecting contention of Southern states that voting qualifications were powers reserved to states. March 7

Hundreds of Black teen-agers rioted in 12-square block area in Watts district of Los, Angeles, California. March 16

United States Supreme Court ruled Virginia poll tax unconstitutional, thereby ending poll tax in three other Southern states. March 25

United States Census Bureau reported Cook County, Illinois, had the largest Black population of any county in the United States: 861,146. March 26

Bill (William F.) Russell named as Boston Celtics basketball coach, first Black to direct major American professional sports team. March 28

First World Festival of Black Arts was held in Dakar, Senegal. April 1-24

Pfc. M.L. Olive was the first Black to receive the Congressional Medal of Honor in the Vietnam War. April 22

John Lewis was defeated for re-election as Chairman of the Student Nonviolent Coordinating Committee (SNCC) by Stokely Carmichael, reflecting SNCC move to deemphasize whites' role in civil rights activities. May 16

White House Civil Rights Conference issued recommendations calling for multi-billion dollar program to give Blacks "true equality." May 25

Eliot P. Skinner confirmed by United States Senate as Ambassador to Upper Volta, Africa. May 29

Stephen J. Wright resigned as President of Fisk University to become President of the United Negro College Fund. June 2

James H. Meredith began 200-mile civil rights march from Memphis, Tennesse to Jackson, Mississippi, to encourage voter registration among Blacks in the South. June 6

Meredith was shot in the back from ambush near Hernando, Mississippi. June 7.

National convention of Congress of Racial Equality (CORE) voted to adopt resolution endorsing concept of "black power" as enunciated by Stokely Carmichael during the Meredith March. July 1.

NAACP disassociated itself from the "Black Power" doctrine. July 4.

Dr. Martin Luther King, Jr., launched drive to make Chicago an "open city." July 10.

Three nights of rioting swept Chicago's West Side Black district. July 12-15.

Shooting, fire-bombing and looting in the Black area of Hough on Cleveland's East Side. July 18-23.

Dr. Martin Luther King, Jr., stoned in Chicago while leading march in Gage Park section of Chicago's Southwest Side. Aug. 5.

New York Assemblyman Percy Sutton elected President of the Borough of Manhattan. Sept. 13.

Emmet T. Rice was appointed United States Alternate-Executive Director of the World Bank. Oct. 18.

Edward W. Brooke elected United States Senator in Massachusetts on the Republican ticket; the first Black Senator since Reconstruction. Nov. 9.

House of Representatives denied Adam Clayton Powell his Congressional seat until Select Committee probed and reported on his qualifications. Jan. 10.

Twenty Governors proclaimed Negro History Week. Feb. 14.

President L. B. Johnson proposed new Federal Civil Rights Act of 1967. Feb. 16.

Nineteen men, including a County Sheriff and KKK Imperial Wizard were indicted under felony provisions of 1870 Civil Rights statute in connection with death of three civil rights workers. March 1.

House of Representatives, 207-116, voted to exclude Adam Clayton Powell. March 2.

The Negro National Business & Professional Committee was organized at the Harvard Club in New York City; consisted of 47 business and professional Black leaders who plan to raise $1,000,000 annually to subsidize the Legal & Education Fund of the NAACP. March 24.

Dr. Martin Luther King, Jr., announced he would take strong stand against Vietnam War because it was major obstacle to Civil Rights movement. March 24.

Texas Legislature passed first civil rights act in recent history. April 6.

Roman Catholic priest Rev. Joseph Groppi charged with

obstructing police and resisting arrest during disturbances following meeting of Milwaukee NAACP Youth Council of which he is advisor. May 7.
Blacks of Roxbury section in Boston rioted in protest against Department of Welfare treatment. June 4.
Blacks rioted in downtown Tampa, Florida, looting and setting block afire; 500 National Guardsmen called in by Governor. June 12.
United States Supreme Court upheld contempt of court conviction of Rev. Dr. Martin Luther King, Jr., and seven other ministers for violating order against leading desegregation protests in Birmingham, Alabama. June 14.
Blacks rioted in Cincinnatti, Ohio; Governor ordered 900 National Guardsmen to join 900 policemen. June 15.
Rev. E. H. Evans nominated for United Church of Christ national secretary, first Black to be nominated. June 24.
Fourteen persons shot, 1500 Black youths rioted in Buffalo, N.Y. June 30.
James Meredith completed second march to Canton, Mississippi, to prove that state and local police can protect Blacks if they choose. July 5.
United States Supreme Court unanimously outlawed antimiscegantion laws. June 12.
United States Senator Edward R. Brooke of Massachusetts received Annual Spingarn Medal of the NAACP for distinguished achievement. July 10.
Band of Blacks rioted in Newark, New Jersey; 11 persons killed. July 13.
SNCC Chairman "Rap" Brown slightly wounded after firey speech in Cambridge, Maryland, urging Blacks to burn town unless Black demands met. July 25.
Thousands of Blacks rioted throughout Detroit, Michigan. July 24.
President L. B. Johnson sent 4,700 army paratroopers into Detroit to deal with rioting. July 25.
National Guard fired on snipers as death toll in Detroit reached 36, more than the number slain in the 1965 Watts riot. July 27.
President Lyndon B. Johnson appointed 11-member committee headed by Governor Otto Kerner of Illinois and Mayor John Lindsay of New York to study causes and propose solutions to racial riots. July 28.
National Guard and United States Army withdrew from Detroit. July 29.
Mrs. Elizabeth D. Koontz was elected President of the National Education Association, the largest professional organization in the world. July.

The Baltimore Afro-American celebrated its 175th anniversary. August.
James Nabrit, Jr., resigned as President of Howard University in Washington, D.C. after a series of confrontations with Black militants on campus.
Carl Stokes was elected Mayor of Cleveland, Ohio. Nov. 9.
Richard G. Hatch was elected Mayor of Gary, Indiana. Nov. 9.
United States Senate confirmed the appointment of Thurgood Marshall as the first Black Associate Justice of the United States Supreme Court. Sept.
President Lyndon B. Johnson signed bill extending life of Civil Rights Commission to January, 1973. Dec. 16.
Maryland Constitutional Convention approved ban on racial discrimination. Dec. 26.
Brandeis University Lemberg Institute of Study of Violence announced that only five of two hundred disturbances that occured in 1967 appeared to have been precipitated by outside agitators. Dec. 29.

1968

About 100 Black leaders representing 20 organizations held a secret meeting in Washington, D.C. and formed a coalition "Black United Front," to organize Blacks in the nation's capital. Jan. 9.
Henry Lewis became the first Black appointed music director of a symphony orchestra in the United States, the New Jersey Symphony. Feb. 15.
For the first time in modern Alabama history, two Black candidates became the party's delegates to the Democratic National Convention. Feb. 26.
The President's National Advisory Commission on Civil Disorders issued its reports on the causes of racial riots in the summer of 1967. March 2.
Affirming a 1966 Federal District Court decision, the United States Supreme Court unanimously ruled that Alabama must desegregate its prisons within a year. The Court rejected Alabama's contention that segregation was necessary to maintain order. March 11.
The first state-wide open-housing law in the South became law in Tennessee after nearly a year of demonstrations in Memphis. March 27.
Black separatists met in Detroit for a National Black Conference sponsored by the Malcolm X Society to "set up an independent Black government" in five Southern states, and to write a "Black Declaration of Independence." March 30.
Martin Luther King, Jr., was assassinated in Memphis,

Tennessee, while preparing a march on behalf of striking sanitation workers. April 4.
Widespread violence struck 125 cities following the assassination of Martin Luther King, Jr.; thirty-eight people were killed and 20,000 arrested. Fifty-thousand Federal and State troops were on duty throughout the country. April 5-11.
President L. B. Johnson declared a day of mourning in honor of Martin Luther King, Jr. April 7.
Mrs. Coretta King, Dr. King's widow, elected to Board of Directors of Southern Christian Leadership Conference (SCLC); Dr. Ralph D. Abernathy was elected president. April 9.
Civil Rights Act of 1968 featuring provisions to eliminate racial barriers in the nation's housing programs was passed by Congress. April 10.
A settlement was reached in the Memphis, Tennessee, sanitation men's strike; the cause that had brought Martin Luther King, Jr., to Memphis where he was assassinated. April 16.
The United States Department of Justice reported that 46 persons had been killed in the rioting that followed the assassination of Martin Luther King, Jr. April 23.
Rev. Ralph D. Abernathy led a "delegation of 100" representatives of minority groups in conferences in Washington, D.C. with Cabinet members and Congressional leaders and presented a list of legislative demands for the poor people of America. April 29.
"Resurrection City," symbol of the Poor People's March on Washington, D.C., was dedicated, May 13.
In three unanimous decisions the United States Supreme Court ruled that "freedom of choice" desegregation plans in the South were inadequate if they did not bring about integration as well as other plans would. Allowing children of all races to choose their schools, a plan practiced in 9 out of 10 Southern communities, tended to perpetuate segregation, declared the Court. May 27.
In a land-mark decision, the United States Supreme Court ruled that racial discrimination was prohibited in all sales and rentals of residential and other property. June 18.
The Fourth Assembly of the World Council of Churches, meeting in Uppsala, Sweden, elected three American blacks to the Central Committee, the body that makes policy between Assemblies. July 18.
N. Y. Times survey of civil rights movement found lack of meaningful progress for blacks had led to ferment in movement and changes in groupings and goals among such groups

as the National Association for the Advancement of Colored People, Congress of Racial Equality, and National Urban League. July 21.

Arthur Ashe became the first American since 1955 to win the United States amateur tennis singles title at the Longwood Cricket Club in Brooline, Mass. Aug. 25.

The Democratic Party Convention had 337 black delegates -- 189 voting, 148 alternates. A Black caucus was convened several times during the convention under the leadership of Rep. John Conyers, Jr. (Michigan) and Mayor Richard G. Hatcher of Gary, Indiana. Aug. 27.

The Rev. Channing E. Phillips of Washington, D.C. was the first Black ever placed in nomination for President of the United States at a major party convention at the Democratic Convention in Chicago. Aug. 28.

Among the resolutions adopted by the 3rd Black Power Conference held in Philadelphia were proposals supporting the organization of a national Black party for "Progressive and radical social change." The Rev. Dr. Nathan Wright was Chairman. Sept. 1.

Arthur Ashe was the first winner of the new United States Open Championship in tennis at Forest Hills Stadium in New York City. Sept. 9.

Attorney General of the United States, Ramsey Clark, announced that there was a drop in the number and severity of riots and disorders in the summer of 1968 compared with data of former years. Clark noted, however, that riots following the death of Martin Luther King, Jr. "made April, 1968, the second worst month in recent years." Oct. 3.

James Earl Jones was hailed as the Broadway theater's newest "star" after the opening of The Great White Hope. Oct. 5.

Two Black athletes, sprinters Tommie Smith and John Carlos, used the victory ceremony of the 200-meter dash at the Games of the 19th Olympiad in Mexico City as a vehicle for a Black Power demonstration (Smith had won a gold medal for the event, Carlos a bronze medal for third place). Oct. 16.

Nine Blacks -- a record -- all Democrats, were elected to the House of Representatives. Nov. 5.

Mrs. Shirley Chisholm defeated James L. Farmer in the Congressional race in the Bedford-Stuyvesant section of Brooklyn, N.Y. to become the first Black woman elected to the House of Representatives. Nov. 5.

Yale University, following a recommendation made by a faculty-student committee including four student members of the University's Black Student Alliance, announced that it would offer a B.A. degree in Afro-American studies. Dec. 12.

1969

The House of Representatives voted to seat Adam Clayton Powell, Congressman from Harlem, fine him $25,000 for alleged mis-use of payroll, and travel funds, and strip him of his 22 years of seniority. Jan. 1.
Charlie Gifford of Charlotte, North Carolina, won the $100,000 Los Angeles Open for $20,000. Gifford was the second man to win a major pro golf tournament. Jan. 12.
U.S. Attorney General Ramsey Clark reported that since the passage of the 1965 Voting Rights Act, voter registration in Alabama, Georgia, Louisiana, and South Carolina had increased from 730,000 to nearly 1,500,000. Jan. 13.
Eldridge Cleaver, a Panther leader sought by the police as a parole violator since November, 1968, remained in hiding as he was inaugurated in absentia in Toronto, Canada, as "president-elect-in-exile" of the United States. Jan. 20.
Roy Campanella was elected to baseball's Hall of Fame by the Baseball Writers Association of America. He is the second Black player to be admitted to the Hall. Jan. 21.
A Black man was appointed to Virginia's State Board of Education for the first time in the State's history when Governor Mills E. Godwin, Jr. appointed Hilary H. Jones to this position. Feb. 1.
James Earl Ray, who pleaded guilty in a Memphis court to murdering Dr. Martin Luther King, Jr., last year, was sentenced to 99 years in prison. March 10.
Former N.Y. Yankee Hector Lopez was appointed manager of the Washington Senators' Buffalo triple A team of the International League. He became the first Black manager in professional baseball. March 20.
A strike of hospital workers -- mostly Black women -- started in Charleston, North Carolina, and turned into a major civil rights movement led by the Southern Christian Leadership Conference. March 20.
The widow of Marine Sgt. Rodney M. Davis, of Macon, Georgia, received the Medal of Honor from Vice-President Spiro Agnew. Davis was killed in 1967, and he was the 10th Black man to receive the award for heroism in Vietnam and the 47th in military history. March 26.
Memorial services for Martin Luther King, Jr. were held throughout the nation. April 4.
The Department of Justice filed its first discrimination suit against a major Southern textile company, charging Cannon Mills with bias in both employment and the rental

of company housing. It marked the first time the government has moved against segregated company-owned housing. April 8.

Clifford L. Alexander, Jr., resigned as chairman of the Equal Employment Opportunity Commission, giving as reason "a crippling lack of administration support." Mr. Alexander is a Black. April 9.

About 100 Black students seized the Student Union building at Cornell University. They emerged the next day carrying 17 rifles and shot guns. April 19.

In South Carolina the Rev. Ralph D. Abernath, successor to Dr. Martin Luther King, Jr., as head of the Southern Christian Leadership Conference, led a march of more than 700 striking Charleston hospital workers. April 22.

The Department of Health, Education, and Welfare told Antioch College that it might operate an all-Black Black Studies section as long as nonblacks were not excluded because of race, color, or national origin. But white students could be excluded on the ground that their background was not "relevant" to the courses. May 2.

James Foreman, director of the National Black Economic Development Conference, demanded that churches and synagogues pay $5,000,000 as reparations to the Black people. May 2.

Howard Lee was elected the first Black mayor of the predominantly (80%) white city of Chapel Hill, North Carolina. May 6.

Black civil rights leader Charles Evers defeated a white incumbent to become mayor of Fayette, Mississippi. May 13.

In a historic ruling the U.S. Supreme Court decided that the House of Representatives violated the Constitution in excluding Harlem Representative Adam Clayton Powell from his seat in the 90th Congress. June 16.

The head of the National Education Association (NEA) Compliance Committee reported that "all but the last step" had been taken to integrate all NEA state affiliates. NEA is the country's largest professional organization. July 2.

The Washington Square United Methodist Church in New York City became the first predominantly white religious organization to give money to the National Black Economic Development Conference by handing the group's chief spokesman, James Foreman, a check for $15,000. July 6.

The Department of Justice intensified its school desegregation efforts by accusing the board of education of Chicago and the state board in Georgia of segregation. The Department contended that Chicago practiced faculty segregation and that Georgia maintained an unconstitutional dual system. July 9.

The strike of nonprofessional hospital workers in Charleston ended after 113 days, having brought organized labor and the civil rights movement together for the first time. July 18.

Presidents of 31 Black colleges ended a 3-day meeting in Mobile, Alabama, by passing a resolution that criticized the federal government's lack of understanding of the role of the 113 predominantly Black colleges in the United States. July 18.

Columbia University announced the election of the first two Blacks to its Board of Trustees, Franklin A. Thomas and Dr. M. M. Weston. July 25.

In a special election held in Greene County, Alabama, Blacks won four of five seats on the county commission and two seats on the five-member school board, which already included one Black. The victory was hailed by the Rev. Ralph D. Abernathy as "the most significant achievement by Black men since the Emancipation Proclamation." July 29.

The defense attorney for Bobby Seale, the Black Panther party's national chairman held in $25,000 bail on charges involving the murder last May of a former Black Panther in Connecticut, accused the Justice Department of initiating a national campaign to harass the party. Aug. 20.

After hearing that political pressures prompted the government to call for a delay in Mississippi school integration, about half of the staff of lawyers in the Justice Department's Civil Rights Division agreed to protest the Nixon Administration's handling of desegregation policies. Aug. 27.

The Episcopal Church's House of Delegates voted to grant James Foreman's Black Economic Development Conference $200,000. The organization had demanded the sum as "reparations." Sept. 3.

Josh White, Black blues and folk singer, died. Sept. 5.

Alabama ended its first week of widespread school integration with no trouble and no resistance from white parents although Governor George Wallace had urged defiance by white parents. Sept. 6.

The U.S. Commission on Civil Rights unanimously charged that the Nixon administration has chosen the wrong school desegregation policy and has made that policy an apparent "major retreat." Sept. 12.

Rex Ingram, veteran Black actor whose career spanned 50 years on Broadway and in films, died. He was best known for his role "De Lawd" in the all-Black 1936 film, <u>The Green Pastures</u>. Sept. 20

The "Philadelphia Plan", which sets minority hiring guidelines for six skilled construction crafts, was ordered into effect by Labor Secretary George P. Shultz on federally assisted projects in Philadelphia. Sept. 23.

The first Black mayor of a major American city, Carl. B. Stokes of Cleveland, won renomination as the Democratic mayorality candidate. In the primary, he defeated his opponent with a greater percentage of votes than he had in the 1967 primary. Sept. 30.

Senator Edward W. Brooke of Massachusetts became the first Senator to ask publicly that President Nixon withdraw the nomination of Clement F. Haynsworth, Jr., to the U.S. Supreme Court.

Dr. Clifton Reginald Wharton, Jr., was appointed President of Michigan State University. Dr. Wharton, an economist from New York City, became the first Black to head a major public and predominantly white university. Oct. 17.

In a unanimous decision that was a setback for the Nixon administration, the Supreme Court ordered an end to all school segregation "at once." In the case of 33 Mississippi school districts, the court's decision replaced the Warren court's doctrine of "all deliberate speed" and dismissed the contention that providing a continuing education should take precedence over enforcing social justice. Oct. 29.

Democratic Mayor Carl B. Stokes, the first Black to be major of a major American city, won reelection in a close race against his Republican opponent. Nov. 4.

Thirty Mississippi school districts were ordered by a federal appeals court to desegregate by December 31 and to use, with some exceptions, federal integration plans. Nov. 6.

The U.S. Senate rejected the nomination of Clement F. Haynsworth, Jr., of South Carolina to the U.S. Supreme Court. Nov. 21.

Police killed Fred Hampton, the Illinois chairman of the Black Panther party, and another Panther leader with a hail of shotgun and pistol fire during a raid on an apartment near the group's headquarters in Chicago. Dec. 4.

1970

James Edwards, Black actor best known for his performance in the 1949 film, <u>Home of the Brave</u>, died in San Diego, California, after a heart attack. Jan. 4.

Four Southern governors (Governors Lester Maddox of Georgia, John J. McKethen of Louisiana, Albert P. Brewer of Alabama, and Claude R. Kirk of Florida) vowed to defy the federal government's plan to implement student busing arrangements in their home states to achieve desegregated school systems. Jan. 10.

William B. Robertson, a public school supervisor, was appointed by Governor Linwood Holton of Virginia, as a key member of his executive staff. This is the first time that a Black served in a Virginia governor's office. Jan. 13.

Integration of school districts in six Deep South States must take place no later than Feb. 1, the Supreme Court ruled. This decision overturned a court appeals ruling allowing a delay until next fall. Jan. 14.

Some cities closed their schools, some governors declared a special day, and many churches held services on the 41st anniversary of the birth of Dr. Martin Luther King, Jr., the murdered civil rights leader. Jan. 15.

President Nixon nominated Judge G. Harrold Carswell of Florida to the U.S. Supreme Court. Carswell is regarded as a racist and conservative. Jan. 19.

The killing of two Black Panthers, one of whom was Fred Hampton, a 21-year-old leader of the party's Illinois chapter, in a predawn police raid in Chicago last December was ruled "justifiable" by a special coroner's jury. Jan. 21.

The National Institute of National Health presented a study on civil disorders which showed that armed white civilians were more widely involved in civil disorders during the last decade than were Blacks. The report was entitled, A Study of Arrest Patterns in the 1960's Riots. Jan. 22.

Col. Daniel Jones Jr., a fighter-pilot who served as commander of U.S. Forces at Wheelers Air Base in Lybia, was nominated for rank of brigadier general. Lieut. General Benjamin O. Davis, Jr., the only other Black general officer in the Air Force, has retired at the same time. Jan. 25.

Seven Black Panthers who survived a police raid last December 4 were indicted on Chicago on attempted murder charges. Jan. 30.

Joseph L. Searles 3d was the first Black man to be proposed for membership on the New York Stock Exchange. Jan. 30.

The deadlines set by federal courts for midterm school integration passed with small impact on the South, as many public school officials ignored the orders or closed their systems temporarily to await further legal development. Feb. 2.

The Senate and the House approved education appropriation

bills containing amendments introduced by Southern opponents of school desegregation. The House bill contained three antibusing and "freedom of choice" amendments designed to restrict federal power to enforce desegregation. The Senate bill contained an amendment which would halt busing of children to achieve racial balance. Feb. 19.

An all-white federal jury acquitted three white Detroit policemen and a Black private guard of conspiring to violate the civil rights of 10 persons in the Algiers Motel, Detroit, in 1967, where three Blacks were found dead. The prosecution charged the men with use of excessive force to obtain information about sniping during the Detroit riots. Feb. 25.

School buses bringing Black children to a newly integrated school in Lamar, South Carolina, were attacked with ax handles and baseball bats by a mob of raging whites. State policemen used tear gas and clubs to drive the whites back. Several children were injured. After the children left, the mob overturned two of the three buses before being dispersed. March 3.

William Warfield, the world-famous singer, celebrated his 20th anniversary debut in New York City concert halls at a recital at Tully Hall in Lincoln Center. March 23.

President Nixon pledged to eliminate officially imposed segregation in Southern schools but said that until he has further court guidance he could not require the elimination of segregation caused by residential patterns. He did, however, announce plans to allocate $1.5 billion to help local schools overcome the effects of residentially caused segregation. March 24.

In an effort to head off a Supreme Court-backed school integration plan, Governor Claude R. Kirk, Jr., of Florida ordered Manatee County pupils to ignore the desegregation order. Kirk also personally assumed control of the county's school system after suspending the school superintendent. April 6.

The U.S. Senate refused to confirm the nomination of Judge G. Harrold Carswell to the Supreme Court in a vote of 51 to 45. April 8.

Governor Kirk of Florida yielded to the authority of a federal court, and announced that he would reinstate the Manatee County school board and direct it to put into effect a court-ordered-integration plan. The court had ordered the governor to pay a $10,000-a-day fine unless he released control of the system. April 12.

Kingman Brewster, Jr., president of Yale University, stated that in his personal opinion that he was "skeptical" as to whether Black revolutionaries could get "a fair trial anywhere in the United States." He said that he was "appalled and ashamed" that such a situation can exist and blamed police action against Black Panthers for it. April 24.

Allison Davis was appointed as John Dewey Distinguished Professor of Education at the University of Chicago, the first Black man to hold a major endowed chair in this or any of the great universities in the United States. April 27.

James H. Hubert, the first executive director of the New York Urban League, died. May 1.

The criminal charges against seven Black Panthers who survived a Chicago police raid in December 1969 in which two Black Panthers were killed were dropped after the prosecution said that there was insufficient evidence that any of the defendants had fired at the police. May 8.

A dusk-to-dawn curfew was imposed on Atlanta, Georgia, after a night of rioting that left six Blacks dead from police fire and at least 75 persons injured. Twelve hundred National Guardsmen surrounded the devastated neighborhood. Governor Lester G. Maddox ordered the Guard to shoot to kill and called the riot a "Communist conspiracy." May 12.

A student at Jackson (Mississippi) State College and a local high school senior, both Blacks, were killed in a barrage of police gunfire that riddled a student dormitory. May 14.

The NAACP gave $50,000 to save a commission set up last December for a national study of clashes between the police and the Black Panthers. May 14.

George C. Wallace was elected again as governor of Alabama in a campaign based upon his historical racism. June 2.

Earl Grant, entertainer and organist who was best known for his instrumental version of "Ebb Tide," died in an automobile crash. June 11.

Federal Judge A. Leon Higginbotham, Jr., was elected a trustee of Yale University, the first Black person to be chosen for the institution's governing board since Yale was founded in 1701. June 15.

Kenneth A. Gibson was elected Mayor of Newark, New Jersey, thus becoming the first Black man to be elected Mayor of a major eastern seabord city. June 16.

Officials of the National Education Association testified before a Senate Committee that 5,000 Black teachers and principals in Southern schools had either been dismissed or demoted as a result of desegregation. June 16.

The Rev. Henry Jogner, Jr. became the minister of the Cavalry Methodist Church in Atlanta, Georgia, the first Black minister to take the pulpit of an all-white Southern parish of the United Methodist Church, a Protestant giant in the "Bible Belt." June 26.

The head of the NAACP, Bishop Stephen G. Spottswood, denounced the Nixon administration as anti-Black in its policies. June 30.

Dr. Felton G. Clark, retired president of Southern University, one of the nation's leading Black educators and a controversial figure in early efforts to integrate lunch counters in Louisiana, died. July 1.

"It's the job of Congress or the courts" to change the legal requirements for school integration if the current laws are insufficient, stated the civil rights chief of the Justice Department before a Senate committee in a defense of administration policy. Democratic members of the committee had attacked the administration's desegregation policy as being a set of narrow legalisms. July 13.

Louis E. Lomax, a nationally known Black writer and member of the faculty of Hofstra University in Long Island, N.Y., was killed in an automobile crash. He was known as one of the major interpreters of the integration movement. Aug. 1.

Arrangements were made for graveside services for a Black soldier killed in Vietnam after a federal judge ordered a segregated cemetery in Fort Pierce, Florida, to accept the body. A 72-year-old whitewoman had donated the grave despite a charter assuring burial only to white plot owners. Aug. 27.

There was no reported violence as most Southern children returned to school, many to newly integrated classrooms. Aug. 31.

Dr. Hugh S. Scott was appointed Superintendent of Schools by the District of Columbia Board of Education. He became the first Black school superintendent of a major American city. Sept. 1.

The killing of two Black students at Jackson State College the past May was "unreasonable unjustified overreaction" on the part of Mississippi policemen, reported the President's Commission on Campus Unrest. Oct. 1.

Dr. Ralph J. Bunche, Under Secretary of the United Nations, received the 8th Annual Family of Man Awards for excellence from the Council of Churches of the city of New York. Oct. 22.

Wilson Riles defeated Superintendent of Public Instruction Max Rafferty in one of the most stunning upsets in California political history to become the first Black man ever to hold statewide office in California. Nov. 4.

A record number of Blacks were elected to the U.S. House

of Representatives. The members elected for the first time were: George W. Collins (Illinois), Ronald V. Dellums (California), Ralph Metcalfe (Illinois), Parren J. Mitchell (Maryland), Charles B. Rangle (New York). All the Representatives are Democrats. Nov. 4.

City Councilman Louis Mason, Jr. became the first black man elected President of Pittsburgh's City Council. Dec. 14.

The Federal Reserve Bank of New York announced the appointment that Whitney M. Young Jr., executive director of the National Urban League, had been appointed by the Federal Reserve Board to a three-year term as a Class C director of the bank. He will be the first Black to serve on the bank's board, although other Blacks are serving on the boards of other regional banks. Dec. 29.

1971

Dr. Melvin H. Evans, a black physician, was installed as the first elected Governor of the Virgin Islands. Jan. 4.

Dr. Leon Howard Sullivan, a Black minister from Philadelphia, was elected to the board of directors of the General Motors Corporation. He is the first Black man to be appointed to the world's largest industrial corporation. Jan. 4.

Louis Armstrong, "King of Jazz," died. July 7.

SELECTED BIBLIOGRAPHY ON THE AFRO-AMERICAN

Adams, Russel L. Great Negroes Past and Present, 3rd ed. (Chicago, Afro-Am Publishing Company, 1970).

American Travelers' Guide to Negro History (American Oil Company, Room 1004, 910 South Michigan Avenue, Chicago, Ill. 60680).

Aptheker, Herbert. A Documentary History of the Negro People in the United States (New York, The Citadel Press, 1968) 2 vols.

Abramson, Doris E. Negro Playwrights in the American Theatre, 1925-59. (New York, Columbia University Press, 1969).

Banks, James A. March Toward Freedom: A History of Black Americans (Palo Alto, Calif., Fearon Publishers, 1970).

Bennett, Lerone, Jr. Before the Mayflower: A History of the Negro in America, 1619-1964 (Baltimore, Penguin Books, 1967).

Bennett, Lerone, Jr. Black Power: USA: The Human Side of Reconstruction, 1867-1877 (Chicago, Johnson Publishing Company, 1967).

Bennett, Lerone, Jr. Pioneers in Protest (Chicago, Johnson Publishing Company, 1968).

Blaustein, Albert P. and Robert L. Zangrando. Civil Rights and the American Negro: A Documentary History (New York, Washington Square Press, 1968).

Bontemps, Arna. editor. American Negro Poetry (New York, Hill & Wang, 1966).

Brink, William J. The Negro Revolution in America (New York, Simon & Schuster, 1964).

Broderick, Francis L. and Meir, August. Negro Protest in the 20th Century (Indianapolis, Bobbs-Merril, 1965).

Burns, W. Heywood. Voices of Negro Protest in America (New York, Oxford University Press, 1963).

Butcher, Margaret Just. The Negro in American Culture. (New York, Mentor Books, 1967).

Carmichael, Stokley. Black Power, The Politics of Liberation in America (New York, Random House, 1967).

Chambers, Bradford, editor. Chronicles of Negro Protest: A Background Book For Young People (New York, Parents Magazine, 1968).

Clarke, John H. American Negro Short Stories (New York, Hill & Wang, 1966).

Courlander, Harold. Negro Folk Music U.S.A. (New York, Columbia University Press, 1963).

Daedalus, The Negro American. Edited and with introductions by Talcott Parsons & Kenneth B. Clark (Boston, Houghton, Mifflin, 1966).

Dorson, Richard M. editor. American Negro Folktales (Greenwich, Conn. Fawcett Publications, 1967).

Dover, Credric. American Negro Art (Greenwich, Conn., New York Graphic Society, 1960).

Drotning, Philip T. A Guide to Negro History (Garden City, N.Y., Doubleday, 1968).

Du Bois, W.E.B. The Souls of Black Folk (New York, Crestm 1961).

Durham, Philip and Jones, Everett L. The Negro Cowboys (New York, Dodd Mead, 1968).

Elkins, Stanley M. Slavery (New York, Gross & Dunlap, 1963).

Filler, Louis. The Crusade Against Slavery (New York, Harper, 1960).

Fishel, Leslie U. Jr., and Benjamin Quarles. The Negro American: A Documentary History (Glenview, Ill., Scott, Foresman, 1967).

Franklin, John Hope. The Emancipation Proclamation (New York, Doubleday, 1963).

Franklin, John Hope. From Slavery to Freedom: A History of Negro Americans (New York, Knopf, 1969).

Franklin, John Hope and Isadore Starr. The Negro in Twentieth Century America: A Reader on the Struggle for Civil Rights (New York, Vintage Books, 1967).

BIBLIOGRAPHY

Frazier, Franklin E. Black Bourgeoisie (New York, Collier, 1962).

Frazier, Franklin E. The Negro Family in the U.S. (Chicago, University of Chicago Press, 1966).

Friedman, Leon, editor. Civil Rights Reader: Basic Documents of the Civil Rights Movement (New York, Walker, 1967).

Garland, Phyl. The Sound of Soul (Chicago, H. Regney Co., 1969)/

Goldston, Robert. The Negro Revolution (New York, Macmillan, 1968).

Gosnell, Harold F. Negro Politicians (Chicago, University of Chicago Press, 1967).

Grant, Joanne, editor. Black Protest: History, Documents and Analyses, 1619-Present (New York, Fawcett World Library, 1968).

Greene, Lorenzo. The Negro in Colonial New England, 1620-1776 (New York, Athenum, 1968).

Hill, Herbert. Anger, And Beyond: The Negro Writer in the United States (New York, Harper & Row, 1966).

Hill, Herbert. editor. Soon, One Morning: New Writing by American Negroes, 1940-62 (New York, Knopf, 1963).

Hughes, Langston. Black Magic; A Pictorial History of the Negro in American Entertainment (Englewood Cliffs, N.J., Prentice-Hall, 1967).

Hughes, Langston and Milton Meltzer. A Pictorial History of the Negro in America (New York: Crown Publishers, 1968).

International Library of Negro Life and History (New York: Publishers Company, 1967, 1968) 10 vols.
  I. Anthology of the American Negro in the Theatre
  II. Historical Negro Biographies
  III. The History of the Negro in Medicine
  IV. I, Too, Am an American -- A Documentary History
  V. Negro Americans in the Civil War
  VI. The Negro in American Literature
  VII. The Negro in Music and Art
  VIII. The Negro in Sports -- The Upsurge
  IX. The Negro in the United States Prior to the Civil War -- On the Road to Freedom
  X. The Negro in the United States Since the Civil War -- Freedom to the Free

Jacobson, Julius, editor. The Negro and the American Labor Movement (Garden City: Anchor Books, 1968).

Jones, Le Roi and Larry Neal, editors. Black-Fire: An Anthology of Afro-American Writing (New York: Morrow, 1968).

Jones, Le Roi. Black Music (New York: Morrow, 1967).

The Journal of Negro History (Published quarterly by the Association for the Study of Negro Life and History, 1538 Ninth Street, N.W., Washington, D.C.).

Katz, William L., General Editor. The American Negro: His History and Literature (New York: Arno Press, 1968) 45 Vols.

Katz, William L., Eyewitness: The Negro in American History (New York: Pitman Pub., Co., 1967).

Katz, William L. Teachers Guide to American Negro History (Chicago: Quandrangle Books, 1968).

King, Martin Luther. Why We Can't Wait (New York: Harper & Row, 1964).

Littlejohn, David. Black on White: A Critical Study of Writing by American Negroes (New York: Grossman, 1966).

Lee, Irvin H. Negro Medal of Honor Men (New York: Dodd, Mead, 1967).

Margolies, Edward. Native Sons: A Critical Study of 20th Century Negro American Authors (Philadelphia, Lippincott, 1968).

McPherson, James M. The Negro's Civil War: How American Negroes Felt and Acted During the War for the Union (New York: Pantheon Books, 1965).

McPherson, James M. The Struggle for Equality: Abolitionists and the Negro in the Civil War and Reconstruction (Princeton, N.J.: Princeton University Press, 1964).

Meir, August. Negro Thought in America, 1880-1915: Racial Ideologies in the Age of Booker T. Washington (Ann Arbor: University of Michigan Press, 1963).

Meir, August and Elliott Rudwick. The Making of Black America, Essays in Negro Life and History (New York: Atheneum, 1969).

Meltzer, Milton. In Their Own Words: A History of the American Negro (New York: Crowell, 1967).

Metcalf, George R. Black Profiles (New York: McGraw-Hill, 1968).

Negro Book Club Newsletter (Published monthly by the Negro History Book Club, 160 West 85th Street, New York, N.Y.).

The Negro Heritage Library (Yonkers, N.Y. Educational Heritage, 1966).

Osofsky, Gilbert. The Burden of Race: A Documentary History of Negro-White Relations in America (New York: Harper & Row, 1967).

Quarles, Benjamin. The Negro in the American Revolution (Chapel Hill: University of North Carolina Press, 1961).

Quarles, Benjamin. The Negro in the Civil War (Boston: Little, 1953).

Quarles, Benjamin. The Negro in the Making of America (New York: Collier Books, 1964).

Rainwater, Lee. The Moynihan Report and the Politics of Controversy, Including the Full Text of "The Negro Family: The Case for National Action," by Daniel P. Moynihan (Cambridge, Mass.: MIT Press, 1967).

Ruchames, Louis, editor. Racial Thought in America: A Documentary History (Amherst: University of Massachusetts, 1969).

Sandburg, Carl. The Chicago Race Riots, July, 1919 (New York: Harcourt, Brace & World, 1969).

Scott, Benjamin. The Coming of the Black Man (Boston: Beacon Press, 1969).

Sloan, Irving J. The Negro in American Encyclopedias (Washington, D.C., American Federation of Teachers, 1970).

Sloan, Irving J. The Negro in Modern American History Textbooks (Washington, D.C.: American Federation of Teachers, 1968).

Sloan, Irving J. Our Violent Past: An American Chronicle (New York: Random House, 1970).

Time-Life Books, The Negro and the City (New York, 1968).

Washington, Joseph R. Black Religion; The Negro & Christianity in the United States (Boston: Beacon Press, 1966).

Wilson, James Q. Negro Politics: The Search for Leadership (Glencoe, Ill.: Free Press, 1960).

ANNOTATED BIBLIOGRAPHIES

Baker, Augusta. Books About Negro Life for Children (New York Public Library, 20 West 43rd Street, New York, N.Y.) 1968.

Integrated School Books (NAACP Special Contribution Fund, 1790 Broadway, New York, N.Y.) 1967.

Interracial Books for Children (Council on Interracial Books for Children, Inc., 9 East 40th Street, New York, N.Y. 10016).

Jackson, Miles M. A Bibliography of Negro History and Culture for Young People (Pittsburgh: University of Pittsburgh Press, 1969).

Miller, Elizabeth W. The Negro in America: A Bibliography (Cambridge, Mass.: Harvard University Press, 1968).

Rollins, Charlemae. We Build Together (National Council of Teachers of English, 508 South 6th Street, Champaign, Ill.) 1967.

Salk, Erwin A. A Layman's Guide to Negro History (New York: McGraw-Hill, 1967).

Welsch, Edwin K. The Negro in the United States: A Research Guide (Bloomington: Indiana University Press, 1966).

HISTORY & LITERATURE COLLECTIONS

1. Tuskegee Institute, Hollis Burke Frissel Library, Washington Collection, Tuskegee, Ala. 11,000 volumes.
2. Philander Smith College Library, 812 W. 13th St., Little Rock, Ark.
3. University of California (Santa Barbara), Wyles Collection, Goleta, Calif. 13,153 volumes. Emphasis primarily on the Negro as a slave, and implications of slavery and the Civil War.
4. Yale University Library, James Weldon Johnson Memorial Collection of Negro Arts and Letters, New Haven, Conn. Manuscripts and pictures.
5. Howard University Library, Negro Collection, Washington, D.C. 70,000 volumes.
6. Paine College, Warren A. Chandler Library, Augusta, Ga. 396 volumes. Shelflist only, especially race problem as it concerned churches in the Old South.
7. Fort Valley State College, Henry Alexander Hunt Memorial Library, Fort Valley, Ga. 861 volumes.
8. Savannah State College Library, Savannah, Ga. 1,000 volumes. Includes pamphlet and clipping file.
9. Johnson Publishing Company Library, 1820 S. Michigan Ave., Chicago, Ill. 2500 volumes. Pictures, photostats, microfilm.
10. Dillard University Library, 2601 Gentilly Blvd., New Orleans, La. Card index on Negroes in New Orleans, from newspapers covering the period 1850-1865.
11. Xavier University Library, Palmetto and Pine St., New Orleans, La. Restricted use, closed August. Manuscripts, maps, pictures, photostats, microfilm.
12. Detroit Public Library, 5201 Woodward, Detroit, Mich. 849 volumes. Includes music, recordings, dance, drama.
13. St. Augustine Seminary Library, Divine Word Seminary, Bay St. Louis, Miss. 500 volumes. Maintained for missionary work among Negroes.
14. Rust College Library, Magee Memorial Library, Holly Springs, Miss. 3,659 volumes. Includes books by Negroes.
15. Tougaloo College, Eastman Library, Tougaloo, Miss.
16. Bronxville Public Library, 201 Pondfield, Bronxville, N.Y. Books presented in honor of Dr. Ralph J. Bunche, for books by and of the Negro.
17. Columbia University Libraries, Special Collections, Alexander Gumby Collection, New York 10027.
18. New York Public Library Branch, Schomburg Collection, 103 W. 135th St., New York 10027. 33,500 volumes. A library of books, periodicals, manuscripts, clippings, pictures, prints, records, and sheet music which attempts to record the entire experience of people of African descent—historical and contemporary. Restricted use: materials must be used on the premises.
19. University of North Carolina, Louis Round Wilson Library, Chapel Hill, N.C.
20. Western Carolina College Library, Cullowhee, N.C.
21. Duke University Library, Durham, N.C.

22. Bennett College, Thomas F. Holgate Library, Greensboro, N.C. 1,481 volumes.
23. Richard B. Harrison Public Library, 214 S. Blount St., Raleigh, N.C. 3,500 volumes. Mimeographed bibliographies available.
24. The Rutherford B. Hayes Library, 1337 Hayes Ave., Fremont, Ohio. 65,000 volumes.
25. Wilberforce University, Carnegie Library, Daniel Alexander Payne Collection, Wilberforce, Ohio. 4,500 volumes. Includes manuscripts and pictures.
26. Lincoln University, Vail Memorial Library, Lincoln University, Penna. 2,900 volumes. Includes African materials.
27. The Free Library of Philadelphia, Social Science and History Department, Negro Collection, Logan Square, Philadelphia, Penna. 900 volumes.
28. Starks Library, Benedict College, Taylor and Harden St., Columbia, S.C. 29204. 28,100 volumes. Includes manuscripts, maps, pictures, slides.
29. Fisk University Library, Erastus Milo Cravath Memorial Library, Nashville, Tenn. 10,000 volumes. Includes manuscript collection. Restricted use: non-circulating.
30. Texas Southern University Library, Heartman Collection, 3201 Wheeler, Houston, Tex. 11,428 volumes. Includes maps and photographs.
31. Hampton Institute, Collis P. Huntington Memorial Library, George Foster Peabody Collection, Hampton, Va. 9,289 volumes.
32. Virginia State College Library, Norfolk Division, 2401 Corprew Ave., Norfolk, Va.
33. Virginia Union University, William J. Clark Library, 1500 Lombardy St., Richmond, Va. 1,650 volumes.

Excerpts From
THREE LANDMARK CIVIL RIGHTS EXECUTIVE ORDERS

1. <u>Executive Order 8802 Reaffirming Policy of Full Participation in the Defense Program by All Persons, Regardless of Race, Creed, Color, or National Origin, and Directing Certain Action in Furtherance of Said Policy.</u>

Whereas it is the policy of the United States to encourage full participation in the national defense program by all citizens of the United States, regardless of race, creed, color, or national origin, in the firm belief that the democratic way of life within the Nation can be defended successfully only with the help and support of all groups within its borders; and

Whereas there is evidence that available and needed workers have been barred from employment in industries engaged in defense production solely because of considerations of race, creed, color, or national origin, to the department of workers' morale and of national unity:

Now, therefore, by virtue of the authority vested in me by the Constitution and the statutes, and as a prerequisite to the successful conduct of our national defense production effort, I do hereby reaffirm the policy of the United States that there shall be no discrimination in the employment of workers in defense industries or government because of race, creed, color, or national origin, and I do hereby declare that it is the duty of employers and of labor organizations, in defense industries, without discrimination because of race, creed, color, or national origin;

And it is hereby ordered as follows:

. . . .
3. There is established in the Office of Production Management a Committee on Fair Employment Practices, which shall consist of a chairman and four other members to be appointed by the President. . . .

June 25, 1941

2. <u>Executive Order 9808 Establishing The President's Committee on Civil Rights</u>.

Whereas the preservation of civil rights guaranteed by the Constitution is essential to domestic tranquility, national security, the general welfare, and the continued existence of our free institutions; and

Whereas the action of individuals who take the law into their own hands and inflict summary punishment and weak personal vengeance is subversive of our democratic system of law enforcement and public criminal justice, and gravely threatens our form of government; and

Whereas it is essential that all possible steps be taken to safeguard our civil rights:

Now, therefore, by virtue of the authority vested in me as President of the United States by the Constitution and the statutes of the United States, it is hereby ordered as follows:

1. There is hereby created a committee to be known as the President's Committee on Civil Rights, which shall be composed of the following-named members, who shall serve without compensation:

. . . .

2. The Committee is authorized on behalf of the President to inquire into and to determine whether and in what respect current law-enforcement measures and the authority and means possessed by Federal, State, and local governments may be strengthened and improved to safeguard the civil rights of the people.

. . . .

5. The Committee shall make a report of its studies to the President in writing, and shall in particular make recommendations with respect to the adoption or establishment, by legislation or otherwise, of more adequate and effective means and procedures for the protection of the civil rights of the people of the United States.

Harry S. Truman

The White House
December 5, 1946

3. Executive Order 9981 Establishing The President's Committee on equality Of Treatment And Opportunity In the Armed Forces.

Whereas it is essential that there be maintained in the armed services of the United States the highest standards of democracy, with equality of treatment and opportunity for all those who serve in our country's defense:

Now, therefore, by virtue of the authority vested in me as President of the United States, by the Constitution and the statutes of the United States, and as Commander in Chief of the armed services, it is hereby ordered as follows:

1. It is hereby declared to be the policy of the President that there shall be equality of treatment and opportunity for all persons in the armed

forces without regard to race, color, religion, or national origin. This policy shall be put into effect as rapidly as possible, having due regard to the time required to effectuate any necessary changes without impairing efficiency or morale.

. . . .

Harry S. Truman

The White House
July 26, 1948

AN OUTLINE OF AFRO-AMERICAN HISTORY

Europeans Colonize the Americas, 1450-1763

I. The role of the Black in Early America

    A. Free, slave, and indentured Negroes on the Spanish, French, Dutch, Portuguese, and British explorations to the New World.
        1. With Pizarro in Peru
        2. With Cortes in Mexico
        3. With Balboa on discovery of the Pacific Ocean
        4. With De Ayllon in Florida
        5. With Coronado in New Mexico
        6. With Certier and Champlain in North America
        7. With the Jesuits in Canada and in the Mississippi Valley
        8. With the French in Louisiana

    B. The Black Explorers
        1. Estavanico ("Little Stephen")
        2. Jean Baptiste Pointe de Sable in Chicago
        3. Nuflio de Olan with Balboa

    C. English, Black, Scotch, Irish, and Herman indentured servants in the New World.

    D. A basis of equality for Blacks from completion of indentureship between 1623-1660 (voted, testified in court, accumulated land, and mingled freely with other people).

    E. A Black slave labor force in the New World.
        1. Rise of Black enslavement due, in part, to failure of making Indians effective slaves.
        2. In parts of Latin America -- mining and agriculture.
        3. In West Indies-- sugar
        4. In Southern colonies-- tobacco, cotton, rice, indigo.

II. The plantation system in the British North American colonies.

    A. Description, development of plantation system.

    B. Causes for growth.

    C. Change from use of indentured servants to slaves.

    D. Life on a plantation for Black slaves.

AFRO-AMERICAN HISTORY - OUTLINE

III. Free Blacks -- in 1790, more than 59,000 free Blacks in the United States, with more than half in the South: farmers, artisans, mechanics, laborers, seafaring men, hatters, shopkeepers, traders, waiters, cooks, hairdressers, domestice servants, and musicians.

Thirteen English Colonies Win Independence, 1763-1783

I. A turning point toward slaves and slavery in some areas.

    A. 1755, the Quakers" position against the importation of slaves.

    B. Natural rights philosophy vs. slavery

    C. Thomas Jefferson's call for the end of all slave trade and slavery in North America (in 1776 he protested because the King did not stop the slave trade).

    D. Stoppage of the slave trade in some states and manumission acts in Pennsylvania, Connecticut, New York, Rhode Island, and New Jersey from 1780-1784.

    E. Slavery forbidden in the Northwest Territory by the Ordinance of 1787.

II. Black participation in the War for Independence (on both English and American sides).

    A. 5,000 Blacks out of 300,000 total American troops.
        1. Crispus Attucks
        2. Salem Poor
        3. Peter Salem
        4. Austin Dabney
        5. Lemuel Haynes
        6. Tack Sisson
        7. Deborah Gannett

    B. The escape of 100,000 Blacks from slavery.

Americans Become a Nation, 1783-1823

I. Government leaders' concern with economic and political stability.

    A. Compromises
        1. The count of slaves (three-fifths of slaves counted as population for basis of representation).
        2. Article I, Section 9, slave trade, until 1808.

B. Growth of banks, corporations, insurance companies, canals, and turnpikes after 1790; "King Cotton".

C. Powerful pro-slavery interests awakened at this time.

II. Development of slavery in the cotton-growing South due to technological changes in the United States and England.

III. Contributions by intellectual Blacks in early United States

    A. Phyllis Wheatley

    B. Benjamin Banneker

    C. Prince Hall

    D. Jupiter Hammon

    E. Gustavus Vassa

IV. Unchanged status of Blacks, slave and free, in spite of the Bill of Rights (1791).

    A. Uncertainty of full civil liberties to free Blacks.

    B. Elimination of three-fifths representation rule and establishment of full citizenship rights to Blacks by Thirteenth and Fifteenth Amendments.

Concern For Human Rights Increases, Yet Slavery Expands, 1823-1860

I. Abolition movement, a part of the Humanitarian trend.

    A. Black leaders
        1. Martin R. Delaney
        2. Henry Highland Garnet
        3. William H. Day
        4. Frederick Douglass
        5. Samuel Cornish
        6. Robert Purvis
        7. William Wells Brown
        8. James W.C. Pennington
        9. Harriet Tubman
        10. F. Ellen Watkins
        11. William Cooper Nell

    B. White leaders
        1. Elijah P. Lovejoy
        2. Wendell Phillips
        3. Sarah and Angeline Grimke
        4. William Lloyd Garrison
        5. Louis and Arthur Tappan
        6. Theodore Dwight Weld
        7. James G. Birney
        8. Harriet Beecher Stowe
        9. John Greenleaf Whittier

AFRO-AMERICAN HISTORY - OUTLINE

II. Insurrections against slavery.

    A. Gabriel Prosser (Gabriel's Revolt) 1800

    B. Denmark Vesey, 1822

    C. Nat Turner (Turner's Rebellion), 1831

    D. John Brown, 1859

III. Religious groups and leaders in the Humanitarian movement.

    A. Quakers, Methodists, Congregationalists, Baptists
       1. Underground Railroad
       2. Schools for Blacks

    B. Many Black ministers, leaders in the abolition movement
       1. Henry Highland Garnet
       2. James W.C. Pennington
       3. Samuel Cornish

IV. Higher education opportunities for Blacks

    A. Avery College for Negroes in Pittsburg, 1852.

    B. Ashman Institute (later Lincoln University) in Pennsylvania, 1854.

    C. Wilberforce College near Xenia, Ohio, 1856.

    D. John Russworm, first Black graduate from Bowdoin, 1862; publisher of first Black newspaper, <u>Freedom's Journal</u>.

    E. Admission of Blacks to Oberlin College in 1830.

    Technology, Business Enterprise, Westward Expansion, And
    Internal Improvements Spur Economic Growth, 1787-1860

I. Industrial East

    A. Increased slavery in the South related to the growth of the manufacturing of cotton cloth.

    B. Free Blacks, not generally employed as were the immigrant factory and industrial labor workers.

II. "King Cotton" South

   A. Slave system, different economic pattern from the rest of the nation.

   B. The South, a region united politically, economically, and socially by slavery.

III. Frontier West

   A. Frontiersmen and miners
      1. James P. Beckworth
      2. Jacob Dodson

   B. Homesteaders
      1. George W. Bush (Puget Sound)
      2. Hiram Young (Independence, Missouri)

   C. Movement westward by settlers holding respective sectional attitudes toward slavery.

IV. Black inventors" contributions in this period.

   A. Louis Temple (standard harpoon for whaling industry)

   B. James Forten (device for handling sails)

   C. Henry T. Blair (patented corn harvester)

   D. Herbert Rillieux (patented evaporating pan in sugar refining).

Slavery Splits The Nation; Reconstruction Fails The Black, 1860-1877

I. Threat to Southern political power due to Republican triumph in 1860 election; nation at the brink of war.

II. The Civil War

   A. Emancipation Proclamation of January 1863.
      1. Support gained from people influenced by the abolitionists
      2. European opinion influenced
      3. Stimulated hope among Black slaves; thousands flocked to Union armies

B. The Black in the Civil War
    1. 180,000 in the Army; 29,000 in the Navy; 40,000 Black deaths; 21 Black recipients of the Congressional Medal of Honor (Joachim Pease and John H. Lawson).
    2. Blacks commissioned as officers in the Union Army
    3. Escape of 100,000 slaves from plantations to headquarters around Washington: a Southern loss; Northern gain.

III. Political, social, civil rights" effects resulting from the Reconstruction Period in the South.

  A. Southerners
    1. Solid South
    2. Hatred and denial of Negro suffrage
    3. Black political leaders in postwar South
    4. The "new industrial elite's" political and economic power
    5. Disregard for law and legal procedures; use of violence and force; the rise of the Ku Klux Klan.

  B. The Blacks
    1. Republicans
    2. Loss of faith in local self-government
    3. Looking to national government for protection
    4. Laborers at the bottom of the scale in urban areas
    5. Propertyless
    6. Sharecroppers, sometimes share tenants
    7. Intensively unemployed in urban areas
    8. Shorn of political power

IV. Education for Blacks, a concern of many in the North and in the South, 1860-1900.

  A. Higher education supported by private funds.
    1. George Peabody
    2. John D. Rockefeller
    3. Andrew Carnegie
    4. William Baldwin, Jr.
    5. Robert C. Ogden

  B. Black educational institutions
    1. Fisk
    2. Atlanta
    3. Tougaloo
    4. Hampton
    5. Shaw
    6. Morehouse

7. Biddle
8. Tuskegee (Booker T. Washington)

C. Open door to Black applicants in Northern colleges and universities; 34 institutions of higher learning established.

D. Education for Black children
    1. Freedmen's Bureau, 1865-1870
       (a) 4,239 free schools for Blacks
       (b) 9,307 teachers
       (c) 247,333 pupils
    2. Julius Rosenwald Fund
       (a) 5, 357 school buildings
       (b) 663, 615 pupils
    3. Education in the new Souther constitutions
    4. George Peabody Fund
       (a) $2,000,000 for public schools for Blacks
       (b) Some money for George Peabody College for teachers, Nashville, Tennessee
    5. Substantial support for education from Blacks themselves: between 1870 to 1899, $70 million in direct and indirect taxes collected for educational purposes
    6. $15 million in tuition and fees paid by Blacks to educational institutions

E. Substandard educational provisions for Black children in the South
    1. 1907-1908, ratio of money spent-- $5.67 for white teachers' salaries; $1 for Black teachers ' salaries
    2. 1929-1930, ratio of money spent-- $6.46 for white teachers' salaries; $1 for Black teachers" salaries.

The Economy And Democracy Grow, 1865-1917

I. Retrenchment of Black political, social, and economic rights in the South

    A. Poll taxes, complicated voting procedures, "grandfather clause," voting disqualifications for Blacks.

    B. Black sharecropper and tenant farmer; lack of economic opportunities in factories of New South.

    C. Rise of racism and Jim Crowism increase of lynchings; new emphasis on doctrine of white supremacy and Black inferiority.
       1. Movement of anti-Black feeling to North and West
       2. Deep inroads by Ku Klux Klan
       3. 3,000 lynchings between 1882-1900

AFRO-AMERICAN HISTORY - OUTLINE

D. <u>Plessy vs. Ferguson</u>

II. Cheap labor supply for Northern industrial plants and mines up to 1914 by Eastern and Southern European immigrants; no place in industry for Blacks until after the stoppage and restriction of immigrants after 1914.

III. Urbanization of the Black after 1910

    A. From the agrarian, unskilled stage to the lowest rung of industrial unskilled laborers.
        1. Excluded from craft unions and skilled jobs
        2. Remained in severe poverty, crowded ghettos, and in state of constant unemployment.

    B. Between 1988 and 1933 both major political parties, more or less, unconcerned about the economic, political, and social conditions of the Black in the South and in the North.
        1. 1,000,000 Black farmers organized in Colored Farmers Alliance and Co-operative Union because of Populists' call for Black political equality.
        2. South and West reaction to this: intensified white supremacy

IV. Black reaction to retrenchment

    A. Niagara Movement, 1905

    B. NAACP, 1909

    C. National Urban League, 1910

    D. Publications: <u>Boston Guardian,</u> 1901; <u>Chicago Defender,</u> 1905; <u>Crisis,</u> 1910

V. Black inventors

    A. Granville T. Woode (patents for air brakes).

    B. Elijah McCoy (automatic machine lubricator).

    C. Jan E. Matzeliger (shoe laster).

    D. Lewis Latimer (made drawings for Bell's telephone: Maxim gun; carbon filament for the Maxim electric lamp; worked in Edison's laboratory).

    E. John P. Parker (screw for tobacco presses and founder of Ripley Foundry and Machine Company).

F. George Washington Carver (scientist, inventor, and educator).

VI. Rise of Black small businessmen

A. Charles Clinton Spaulding (North Carolina Mutual Life Insurance Company)

B. Some Black banks, grocery stores, drugstores, lumber mills, small construction businesses; beauty culture business (Sarah Spencer, Madam Walker, A.E. Malone).

The Nation Takes A Part In World Affairs, 1865-1930

I. The Black in national defense

A. Black unites organized as part of the regular military establishment
   1. 9th Cavalry, 1886
   2. 10th Cavalry, 1866
   3. 24th Infantry, 1869
   4. 25th Infantry, 1869

B. Blacks serve in the Spanish-American War

C. 350,000 Blacks in the armed forces in World War I

D. 200,000 Blacks served overseas in World War I, both as combat and noncombat troops.

II. The Black in diplomacy

A. Ebenezer D. Bassett, Minister Resident and Consul General in Haiti, 1869.

B. James M. Turner, Minister Resident and Consul General in Liberia, 1871

C. Henry Highland Garnet, Minister Resident and Consul General in Liberia, 1882.

III. Harlem "Renaissance"

The Nation Suffers Depression And War, 1930-1945

I. The Depression, as it affected the Black

AFRO-AMERICAN HISTORY - OUTLINE

A. The Black, the first to be fired and the last to be hired

B. Unemployment
    1. By 1933 one of every four Blacks on relief
    2. Blacks, 3,000,000 out of 18 million on relief

C. Animosity toward Blacks because of competition for jobs

D. Communist propaganda not effective with Blacks in spite of severe hardships

II. The New Deal

A. The social Security Act of 1935, most significant New Deal measure for Blacks
    1. Old-age benefits to workers
    2. Unemployment insurance
    3. Aid to the blind and crippled
    4. Aid to dependent mothers and children
    5. Aid to destitute old people

B. Low-cost housing activities
    1. Decrease in crowded conditions of Black families
    2. Better housing in more than twenty-five cities

C. The Civilian Conservation Corps' Black enrollment in May of 1935, 16,000

D. Aid to Black farmers
    1. Bankhead-Jones Farm Tenant Act, 1937
    2. Farm Security Administration rehabilitation loans

E. Wagner Labor Relations Act, 1935

    1. Steel, coal, iron, mine, electric, garment, and auto workers in industrial unions
    2. 210,000 Blacks in industrial unions (C.I.O.) in 1940 membership

III. World War II and the Black

A. Wartime focus on Blacks' place in the military and in industry
    1. Uncertainty about Black rights because of discrimination during and after World War I

90   BLACKS IN AMERICA

        2. Contradiction over discrimination at home and in the military and over the struggle against Nazi and Fascist racial superiority dogma.

    B. End of discrimination in defense industries, 1941

    C. Beginning of integration of ground troops, 1945

    D. 1,000,000 Black men and women in uniforms, including 6,000 officers

IV. The United Nationa

    A. "All human beings are born free and equal in dignity and rights." (Universal Declaration of Human Rights)

    B. Most prominent American Black participants at formation of United Nations, June 1945
        1. Ralph Bunche
        2. Mary McLeod Bethune
        3. W.E.B. DuBois

    C. Charter provision of United Nations appealing to Blacks: "Respect for human reights and fundamental freedoms for all without distinction as to race, sex, languages, or religion."

      American Deal With Economic Growth, The War On Poverty,
          Civil Rights, World Problems, 1946-Present

I. Expanding civil rights

    A. Truman's Civil Rights Commission, 1946

    B. Truman's executive order integrating armed forces, 1948

    C. <u>Brown vs. The Board of Education</u>, 1954
        1. A reversal of <u>Plessy vs. Ferguson</u>
        2. An outlawing of racial discrimination in the public schools

    D. Civil rights laws
        1. The Civil Rights Law, 1957
        2. The Civil Rights Law, 1960
        3. Initiation by Congress of the Twenty-Fourth Amendment, 1962
        4. The Civil Rights Act, 1965

AFRO-AMERICAN HISTORY - OUTLINE 91

II. Southern reaction and violence to progress in civil rights laws

    A. Resistance to civil rights laws
        1. Little, Rock, Arkansas
        2. Montgomery, Alabama
        3. Oxford, Mississippi
        4. Birmingham, Alabama
        5. Philadelphia, Mississippi

    B. Renewed activities by the Ku Klux Klan

    C. Token compliance toward integration in Southern schools
        1. In Southern states, Blacks in school with whites, 1.18%
        2. In border states, Blacks in school with whites, 54.8%

    D. Apathy of Southerners to acts of violence against Blacks

III. In behalf of civil rights

    A. Protestants

    B. Catholics

    C. Jewish organizations

    D. National Association for the Advancement of Colored People, Roy Wilkins

    E. National Urban League, Whitney M. Young

    F. Student Nonviolent Coordinating Committee, James Forman, John Lewis, Stokely Carmichael

    G. Congress of Racial Equality, James Farmer, Floyd McKissick

    H. A.F.L.-C.I.O.

    I. Conference of Federated Organizations

    J. Southern Christian Leadership Conference, the Rev. Dr. Martin Luther King

IV. Nationalists

    A. Black Muslims, Elijah Muhammad

    B. Organization of Afro-American Unity, Malcolm X.

V. Desperation

    A. Percent distribution of white and Black employed by occupational fields, 1910-1970

    B. Income comparison of whites and nonwhites

    C. Political (voting registration in Southern states in 1959 and 1964 indicates some slight improvements)

    D. Social (stereotypes about Blacks false and incriminating; permeate much of the white community; cause discrimination in housing and in educational opportunities)

VI. Black reaction regarding

    A. Riots in Rochester, Philadephia, New York City, Los Angeles, Chicago

    B. Optimism (almost 75% of Blacks questioned replied that they thought white attidtudes toward them would be better in the next five years)

VII. Federal Government's acts of intervention

    A. Federal troops in Little Rock, in University, Alabama

    B. Nationalized Guard in Oxford, Mississippi

    C. Department of Justice, Federal Bureau of Investigation, federal voting registrars

DISCOGRAPHY

Afro-American Folk Music in the United States

General Collections

Music From the South, recorded in southern states by Frederic Ramsey, Jr., Folkways Records FA 2650, 2651, 2652, 2653, 2654, 2655, 2656, 2657, 2658, 2659. Ten volumes of extremely valuable source material with notes by the collector.

Afro-American Spirituals, Work Songs, and Ballads, recorded in southern states by John, Ruby T., and Alan Lomax and Ruby Pickens Tartt. Library of Congress AAFS-L3.

Negro Folk Music of Alabama, recorded in Alabama and Mississippi by Harold Courlander, Ethnic Folkways Library FE 4417, 4417, 4471, 4472, 4473, 4473. Six volumes of valuable source material, with notes by the collector.

Folk Music U.S.A., compliled by Harold Courlander, Ethnic Folkways Library FE 4530. Two record set, with notes by Charles Edward Smith.

Sounds of the South, recorded by Alan Lomax, Atlantic Recording 1346.

American Folk Music, Vols. II and III, compiled by Harry Smith, Folkways Records FA 2952, 2953. A general collection containing good Negro examples.

Religious

Negro Religious Songs and Services, recorded in southern states by Harold Spivacke, John A., Ruby T., and Alan Lomax, and Lewis Jones, Library of Congress AAFS-L10. Edited by B.A. Botkin,

Spirituals With Dock Reed and Vera Hall Ward, recorded in Alabama by Harold Courlander, Folkways Records FA 2038.

Urban Holiness Service, Elder Charles D. Beck, Folkways Records FR 8901.

Georgia Street Singer, Rev. Pearly Brown, Folk-Lyric FL 108.

Harlem Street Singer, Blind Gary Davis, Prestige 1015.

Blind Willie Johnson, edited by Samuel B. Charters, Folkways FG 3585.

Spirituals, the Gospel Keys (Mother Sally Jones and Emma Daniel), Disc Records 657.

Negro Church Music, recorded by Alan Lomax, Atlantic Recording 1351.

Work Songs

Negro Work Songs and Calls, recorded by John A., Ruby T., and Alan Lomax, Herpert Halpert, and Mary Elizabeth Barnicle, Library of Congress AAFS-L8.

Negro Prison Camp Worksongs, recorded in Texas by Toshi and Peter Seeger, John Lomax, Jr., Chester Bower, and Fred Hollerman, Ethnic Folkways Library FE 4475. Notes by Peter Seeger.

Negro Prison Songs, recorded in Mississippi by Alan Lomax, Tradition Records TLP 1020.

Bands and Street Music

American Skiffle Bands, recorded in southern states by Samuel B. Charters, Folkways Records FA 2610.

One Man Band, Paul Blackman, Folkways Records FA 2605.

Sonny Terry's Washboard Band, Folkways Records FA 2006.

The Music of New Orleans--Music of the Streets, recorded by Samuel B. Charters, Folkways Records FA 2461.

The Music of New Orleans--The Eureka Brass Band, recorded by Samuel B. Charters, Folkways Records FA 2462.

Blues and Related Materials

Lightnin' Hopkins, recorded by Samuel B. Charters, Folkways Records FS 3882

Lightnin' Hopkins: Country Blues, Tradition Records TLP 1035.

Autobiography in Blues, Lightnin' Hopkins, Tradition Records TLP 1040.

The Country Blues of John Lee Hooker, Riverside Records 12-838.

The Country Blues, compiled by Samuel B. Charters, RBF Records RF1.

DISCOGRAPHY

<u>Cat-Iron Sings Blues and Hymns</u>, recorded by Frederic Ramsey, Jr., in Mississippi, Folkways Records FA 2389.

<u>Angola Prisoners' Blues</u>, recorded by Harry Oster and Richard Allen in Louisiana, Louisiana Folklore Society. Notes by Harry Oster and Paul B. Crawford.

<u>Afro-American Blues and Games Songs</u>, recorded in southern states and New York by John A., Ruby T., and Alan Lomax, Ruby Pickens Tartt, Bess Lomax, and John Work, Library of Congress AAFS-L4.

<u>Snooks Eaglin, New Orleans Street Singer,</u> recorded by Harry Oster, Folkways Records FA 2476.

<u>Negro Folk Songs and Tunes,</u> played on guitar and banjo by Elizabeth Cotten, Folkways Records FG 3526.

<u>The Blues Roll On,</u> recorded by Alan Lomax, Atlantic Records 1352.

<u>Roots of the Blues</u>, recorded by Alan Lomax, Atlantic Records 1348.

<u>On the Road,</u> Sonny Terry, J.C. Burris, Sticks McGhee, Folkways Records FA 2369.

<u>Get On Board,</u> Sonny Terry, Brownie McGhee, Coyal McMahan, Folkways Records FA 2028.

<u>The Rural Blues: A Study of the Vocal and Instrumental Sources,</u> edited by Samuel B. Charters, RBF Records RF2.

<u>Brownie McGhee, Blues,</u> Folkways Records Fa 2030.

<u>Blues With Big Bill Broonzy, Sonny Terry, Brownie McGhee,</u> interviewed by Studs Terkel. Folkways Records FS 3817.

<u>Big Bill Broonzy,</u> interviewed by Studs Terkel. Folkways Records FG 3586. Introductory notes by Charles Edward Smith.

<u>Blues in the Mississippi Night,</u> recorded by Alan Lomac, United Artists 4027

<u>Odetta at the Gates of Horn,</u> Tradition Records 1025.

<u>Classical Folk-Blues by Blind Lemon Jefferson,</u> Riverside Records RLP12-125.

Miscellaneous
<u>Jazz, Vol. I - The South,</u> compiled and edited by Charles Edward Smith,

Folkways Records FJ 2801.

Jazz, Vol II. - the Blues, compiled and edited by Frederic Ramsey, Jr., Folkways Records FJ 2802.

Footnotes to Jazz, Vol. I- Baby Dodds, Folkways Records FJ 2290.

Leadbelly's Last Sessions, Vols. I and II, recorded by Frederic Ramsey Jr., Folkways Records FA 2941, 2942.

If He Asks You Was I Laughin', recorded by Tony Schwartz, privately pressed.

Street Cries and Creole Songs of New Orleans, Adelaide Van Wey, Folkways Records FA 2202.

Ring Games, Line Games and Play Party Songs of Alabama, recorded by Harold Courlander, Folkways Records FC 7004.

PREDOMINANTLY BLACK COLLEGES & UNIVERSITIES

Four-year, regionally accredited black-dominated
colleges and universities in the United States.

States and Institutions	Location	Year Founded	Denominational Connection	Enrollment
ALABAMA:				
Alabama A. & M. College	Normal	1875	Non-sect.	1,910
Alabama State Teachers College	Montgomery	1874	Non-sect.	1,886
Oakwood College	Huntsville	1896	Seventh Day Adv.	500
Stillman College	Tuscaloosa	1876	Pres. U.S.A.	698
Talladega College	Talladega	1867	Cong. Christian	578
Tuskegee Institute	Tuskegee	1881	Non-Sect.	2,905
ARKANSAS:				
A. M. & N. College	Pine Bluff	1873	Non-sect.	1,866
Philander Smith College	Little Rock	1868	Methodist	555
Shorter College	N. Little Rock	1886	A.M.E.	731
DELAWARE				
Delaware State College	Dover	1891	Non-sect.	899
DISTRICT OF COLUMBIA:				
Howard University	Washington	1867	Non-sect.	5,580
District of Columbia Teachers College	Washington	1851	Non-sect.	1,357
FLORIDA:				
Bethune-Cookman College	Daytona Beach	1904	Methodist	948
Florida A. & M. College	Tallahassee	1887	Non-sect.	3,367
GEORGIA:				
Albany State College	Albany	1903	Non-sect.	1,619
Clark College	Atlanta	1869	Methodist	1,004
The Fort Valley State College	Fort Valley	1895	Non-sect.	1,091
Morehouse College	Atlanta	1867	Baptist	1,007
Morris Brown College	Atlanta	1881	A.M.E.	1,267
Paine College	Augusta	1883	Methodist & C.M.E.	717
Savannah State College	Savannah	1890	Non-sect.	1,646
Spelman College	Atlanta	1881	Baptist	909
KENTUCKY:				
Kentucky State College	Frankfort	1886	Non-sect.	1,193
LOUISIANA:				
Dillard University	New Orleans	1933	Methodist Cong.	910
Grambling College	Grambling	1801	Non-sect.	3,489
Southern University	Baton Rouge	1880	Non-sect.	1,138
Xavier University	New Orleans	1925	R.C.	1,190
MARYLAND:				
Coppin State Teachers College	Baltimore	1900	Non-sect.	645
Maryland State College	Princess Ann	1886	Non-sect.	644
Morgan State College	Baltimore	1867	Non-sect.	3,552

States and Institutions	Location	Year Founded	Denominational Connection	Enrollment
MISSISSIPPI:				
Alcorn A. & M. College	Alcorn	1871	Non-sect.	2,310
Jackson College	Jackson	1877	Baptist	3,507
Tougaloo College	Tougaloo	1869	Cong.	646
MISSOURI:				
Lincoln University	Jefferson City	1866	Non-sect.	1,888
NORTH CAROLINA:				
A. & T. College of North Carolina	Greensboro	1891	Non-sect.	3,005
Barber-Scotia College	Concord	1867	Preb. U.S.A.	581
Bennett College	Greensboro	1873	Methodist	709
Elizabeth City State Teachers College	Elizabeth City	1891	Non-sect.	864
Fayetteville State Teachers College	Fayetteville	1887	Non-sect.	1,192
Johnson C. Smith University	Charlotte	1867	Presb.	1,408
Livingstone College	Salidbury	1879	A.M.E.Z.	636
North Carolina College	Durham	1910	Non-sect.	2,672
St. Augustine College	Raleigh	1867	Prof. Epis.	991
Shaw University	Raleigh	1865	Baptist	1,049
Winston-Salem Teachers College	Winston-Salem	1892	Non-sect.	1,161
OHIO:				
Central State College	Wilberforce	1887	Non-sect.	2,054
Wilberforce University	Wilberforce	1856	A.M.E.	1,108
OKLAHOMA:				
Langston University	Langston	1897	Non-sect.	1,336
PENNSYLVANIA:				
Lincoln University	Lincoln Univ.	1854	Non-sect.	957
SOUTH CAROLINA:				
Benedict College	Columbia	1870	Baptist	1,255
Claflin University	Orangebury	1869	Methodist	736
South Carolina State College	Orangeburg	1896	Non-sect.	1,689
Voorhees College	Denmark	1897	Prot. Epis.	223
TENNESSEE:				
Fisk University	Nashville	1865	Non-sect.	1,128
Knoxville College	Knoxville	1875	Presb.	854
Lane College	Jackson	1882	C.M.E.	1,008
LeMoyne College	Memphis	1870	Cong. Christian A.M.E. Assn.	621
Tennessee State University	Nashville	1919	Non-sect.	4,318
TEXAS:				
Bishop College	Marshall	1880	Baptist	1,656
Jarvis Christian College	Hawkins	1912	Disciples of Christ	537
Prairie View A. & M.	Prairie View	1876	Non-sect.	3,419
Texas Southern University	Houston	1947	Non-sect.	3,330
Wiley College	Marshall	1873	Methodist	677

BLACK COLLEGES AND UNIVERSITIES

States and Institutions	Location	Year Founded	Denominational Connection	Enrollment
VIRGINIA:				
Hampton Institute	Hampton	1868	Non-sect.	2,314
St. Paul's College	Lawrenceville	1888	Episcopal	447
Virginia State College	Petersburg	1882	Non-sect.	2,104
Virginia Union University	Richmond	1865	Baptist	1,409
WEST VIRGINIA:				
Bluefield State College	Bluefield	1895	Non-sect.	1,102
W. Virginia State College	Institute	1891	Non-sect.	2,008

STATE AGENCIES WITH CIVIL RIGHTS RESPONSIBILITIES

STATE	TOTAL POPULATION	NON-WHITE POPULATION	LAWS*	NAME OF AGENCY	EXECUTIVE OFFICER	ADDRESS AND TELEPHONE
ALASKA	273,000	55,000 (23.7%)	E H A	Alaska State Commission for Human Rights	Willard L. Bowman	520 MacKay Buidling 338 Denali St.,, Anchorage 99501 Tel: 272-9504
ARIZONA	1,302,161	325,540 (25%)	E A	Arizona Civil Rights Commission	Wilbur R. Johnson	1623 W. Washington St. Phoenix, 85007 Tel: (602) 271-5263
CALIFORNIA	18,815,000 (as of 1963)	3,438,023 (18.2%)	E H A	California Fair Employment Practices Commission	Peter R. Johnson	455 Golden Gate Ave. San Francisco 94102 Tel: (415)557-2000)
COLORADO	2,072,000	87,821 (4.2%)	E H A	Colorado Civil Rights Commission	James F. Reynolds	312 State Services Bldg. 1525 Sherman St. Denver 80203 Tel: (303) 892-2621
CONNECT-ICUT	2,975,000	190,000 (15.65%)	E H A	Commission on Human Right & Opportunities	Arthur L. Green	90 Washington St. Hartford 06106 Tel: (203) 566-3350
DELAWARE	589,810	89,180 (15.1%)	E A	Department of Labor and Industrial Relations Division Against Discrimination	Ernest J. Camoriano, Jr.	506 West 10th Street Wilmington 19801 Tel: (302) 658-9251
DISTRICT OF	808,000	509,040 (63%)	E H A	District of Columbia Human Relations Commission	James C. Slaughter	Room 5, District Bldg. 14th and E. Street N.W. 20004 Tel:(202) 629-4723
HAWAII	792,444	571,828 (72.2%)	E H	Department of Labor and Industrial Relations	Robert K. Hasegawa	825 Mililani St. Honolulu 96813 Tel: 548-2211

*This column indicates if state has a law against discrimination in employment(E), private schools and colleges(S), housing not receiving public funds (H), public accommodations (A).

CIVIL RIGHTS AGENCIES 101

STATE	TOTAL POPULATION	NON-WHITE POPULATION	LAWS*	NAME OF AGENCY	EXECUTIVE OFFICER	ADDRESS AND TELEPHONE
IDAHO	792,444 (1960 census)	571,828 (.014%)	E A	Department of Labor	W.L. Robinson	Industrial Administration Building 317 Main Street, Boise 83702 Tel: (208) 344-5811
ILLINOIS	10,893,000	1,070,906 (10%)	E A	Illinois Commission on Human Relations	Roger W. Nathan	160 North LaSalle St. Chicago 60601 Tel: (312) F16-2000 ext. 583
INDIANA	5,000,000	375,000 (7%)	ESHA	Indiana Civil Rights Commission	C. Lee Crean, Jr.	1004 State Office Bldg. Indianapolis, 46204 Tel: (317) 633-4855
IOWA	2,757,537	28,828 (1.05%)	E H A	Iowa Civil Rights Commission	Alvin Hays, Jr.	State Capitol Bldg. Des Moines 50319 Tel: (515) 281-5129
KANSAS	2,178,611	99,945 (4.12%)	E A	Kansas Commission on Civil Rights	Homer C. Floyd	Rm. 1155 W. State Office Bldg. Topeka 66612 Tel: (913) 296-3206
KENTUCKY	3,038,156	215,949 (7.3%)	E A	Kentucky Commission on Human Rights	Galen Martin	Mammoth Life Bldg. 600 West Walnut St. Louisville 40203 Tel: (502) 564-3550

*This column indicates if state has a law against discrimination in employment (E), private schools and colleges (S), housing not receiving public funds (H), public accomodations (A).

STATE	TOTAL POPULATION	NON-WHITE POPULATION	LAWS*	NAME OF AGENCY	EXECUTIVE OFFICER	ADDRESS AND TELEPHONE
MAINE	969,265 (1960 census)	6,056 (.62%)	E H A	Department of Labor and Industry	Miss Marion E. Martin	Rm. 413, State Office Bldg. Augusta 04330 Tel:(207) 289-3331
MARYLAND	3,100,689 (1960 census)	526,770 (17%)	E H A	Maryland Commission on Human Relations	Treadwell O. Phillips	301 West Preston St. Baltimore 21201 Tel: (617) 727-3990
MASSACHU- SETTS	5,295,281	150,209 (2.87%)	E S H A	Massachusetts Commission Against Discrimination	Walter H. Nolan	120 Tremont St. Boston 0218 Tel: (617) 727-3990
MICHIGAN	8,584,000	891,000 (10.4%)	E S H A	Michigan Civil Rights Commission	Burton I. Gordin	1000 Cadillac Square Bldg. Detroit 48226 Tel: (313) 222-1810
MINNESOTA	3,413,864 (1960 census)	42,261 (1.2%)	E S H A	Department of Human Rights	Thomas J. Donaldson	60 State Office Bldg. St. Paul 55101 Tel: (612) 221-2931
MISSOURI	4,319,813	396,846 (9%)	E A	Missouri Commission on Human Rights	Richard E. Risk	Box 1129 314 East High St. Jefferson City 65101 Tel: (314) 635-7961

*This column indicates if state has a law against discrimination in employment(E), private school s and colleges (S), housing not receiving public funds (H), public accommodations (A).

CIVIL RIGHTS AGENCIES

STATE	TOTAL POPULATION	NON-WHITE POPULATION	LAWS*	NAME OF AGENCY	EXECUTIVE OFFICER	ADDRESS AND TELEPHONE
MONTANA	694,000	unavailable	E A	Department of Labor and Industry	Sidney G. Smith	1336 Helena Ave. Helena 59601 Tel: (406) 449-3472
NEBRASKA	1,416,000	53,000 (2.6%)	E A	Nebraska Equal Opportunity Commission	Emmet J. Dennis, Jr.	P.O. Box 4862 State Capitol Bldg. Lincoln 68502 Tel: (314) 473-1624
NEVADA	500,000	40,000 (11.5%)	E A	Nevada Commission on Equal Rights of Citizens	Tyrone K. Leiv	Rm. 100-B, State Bldg. 215 East Bonanza Las Vegas 89101 Tel: (702) 385-0104
NEW HAMPSHIRE	607,000 (1960 census)	2,600 (.4%)	E H A	Commission for Human Rights	Marsha Macey	State House Concord 03301 Tel: (630) 271-2767
NEW JERSEY	7,000,000	700,000 (10%)	E S H A	New Jersey Division of Civil Rights, Department of Law and Public Safety	James H. Blair	1100 Raymond Blvd. Newark 07102 Tel: (201) 648-2700
NEW MEXICO	951,023	344,382 (36.2%)	E A	Human Rights Commission of New Mexico	Byron L. Stewart	1015 Tijeras, N.W. Albuquerque, 87501 Tel: (505) 842-3122

*This column indicates if state has a law against discrimination in employment (E), private schools and colleges (S), housing not receiving public funds (H), public accommodations (A).

BLACKS IN AMERICA

STATE	TOTAL POPULATION	NON-WHITE POPULATION	LAWS*	NAME OF AGENCY	EXECUTIVE OFFICER	ADDRESS AND TELEPHONE
NEW YORK	18,072,089	1,834,026 (10.1%)	E S H A	New York State Division of Human Rights	John C. Clancy	270 Broadway New York City 10007 Tel: (212) 488-7610
NORTH CAROLINA	5,000,000	1,250,000 (25%)	none	North Carolina Good Neighbor Council	D.S. Coltrane	P.O. Box 12525 Raleigh, N.C. 27205 Tel: (919) 829-7996/3354
OHIO	10,749,221	879,861 (8.2%)	E H A	Ohio Civil Rights Commission	Ellis L. Ross	240 Parsons Avenue Columbus 43215 Tel:(614) 469-2785
OKLAHOMA	2,328,284 (1960 census)	220,384 (9.5%)	none	Oklahoma Human Rights Commission	William Y. Rose	P.O. Box 53004 Oklahoma City 73105 Tel: (405) 521-2360
OREGON	1,768,687 (1960 census)	36,650 (2.1%)	E H A	Civil Rights Division, Oregon Bureau of Labor	Russell O. Rogers	466 State Office Bldg. Portland 97201 Tel:(503)226-2161 ext.557
PENNSYLVANIA	11,319,366 (1960 census)	865,362 (7.6%)	E S H A	Pennsylvania Human Relations Commission	Milo A. Manly	100 North Cameron St. Harrisburg 17001 Tel: (717) 787-5010
RHODE ISLAND	859,488 (1960 census)	20,776 (2.4%)	E H A E	Rhode Island Commission for Human Rights	Donald D. Taylor	244 Broad St. Providence 02903 Tel: (401) 521-7100 ext. 6612 or 6613.

*This column indicates if state has a law against discrimination in employment (E), private schools and colleges (S), housing not receiving public funds (H), public accommodations (A).

CIVIL RIGHTS AGENCIES

STATE	TOTAL POPULATION	NON-WHITE POPULATION	LAWS*	NAME OF AGENCY	EXECUTIVE OFFICER	ADDRESS AND TELEPHONE
TENNESSEE	4,000,000	600,000 (15%)	none	Tennessee Commission for Human Development	Cornelius Jones	C3-305 Cordell Hull Bldg Nashville 37219 Tel: (615)741-2424
TEXAS	9,579,677 (1960 census)	2,836,584 (29.6%)	none	Good Neighbor Commission of Texas	Glenn E. Garrett	P.O. Drawer E Austin 78711 Tel: (512) 475-3581
UTAH	1,000,000	10,000 (1%)	E A	Anti-Discrimination Division, Industrial Commission of Utah	John R. Schone	Rm. 418, State Capitol Bldg. Salt Lake City 84114 Tel: (801) 328-5552
VERMONT	439,000	500 (0.1%)	E H A	State Attorney General's Office	James Jeffords	State House Montpelier 05602 Tel: (802) 223-2311
WASHINGTON	3,000,000	16,000 (5.33%)	E S A	Washington State Board Against Discrimination	Alfred E.	1411 Fourth Ave. Bldg. Seattle 98101 Tel: (206) MU2-4594
WEST VIRGINIA	1,860,421 (1960 census)	89,378 (4.8%)	E A	West Virginia Human Rights Commission	Carl W. Glatt	P&G. Bldg. 2019 E. Washington St. Charleston 25305 Tel: (304) 348-2616

*This column indicates if state has a law against discrimination in employment (E), private schools and colleges (S0, housing not receiving public funds (H), public accommodations (A).

STATE	TOTAL POPULATION	NON-WHITE POPULATION	LAWS*	NAME OF AGENCY	EXECUTIVE OFFICER	ADDRESS AND TELEPHONE
WISCONSIN	4,000,000	117,127 (2.9%)	E H A	Equal Rights Division, Department of Industry, Labor and Human Relations	Clifton H. Lee	4802 Sheboygan Ave. Madison 53702 Tel: (608) 266-3131
WYOMING	318,000	6,900 (2.16%)	E A	Department of Labor and Statistics	Paul H. Bachman	304 State Capitol Bldg. Cheyenne 82001 Tel: (307)777-7261/7262

*This column indicated if state has a law against discrimination in employment (E), private schools, and colleges (S), housing not receiving public funds (H), public accommodations (A).

MAJOR BLACK AMERICAN ORGANIZATIONS

Alpha Kappa Alpha Sorority *f: 1908   m: 40,000
to encourage high scholastic and ethical standards, promote unity among college women and to be of service to mankind.

Alpha Kappa Mu Honor Society f: 1937   m: 6,680
encourage high scholarship among college undergraduates and scholarly achievement among the alumni.

Alpha Phi Alpha Fraternity f: 1906   m: 8,000
to develop a strong unit of college trained men dedicated to social uplift and progress through education, active citizenship and the creation of a climate of good-will.

American Teachers Association f: m: 37,000
to provide equal educational opportunities for all children and equality of professional status for all teachers.

Ancient and Accepted Scottish Rite Masons f: 1864   m: 20,000
dedicated its program to fraternal and charitable causes, with emphasis on civic and educational activities.

Ancient Egyptian Arabic Order Nobles of the Mystic Shrine f: m: 24,000
to enhance the work and programs of Prince Hall Masonry, promoting local and national charitable, civic, educational and economic development programs.

Benevolent Protective Order of Reindeer (Women's Auxiliary) f: 1923   m: 3,000
guided by its cardinal principles of "Service, Unity and Charity," participate in a program designed to implement these objectives.

Bible Way Church of Our Lord Jesus Christ World Wide f: 1957   m: 50,000
to promote Christian Fellowship, Pentecostal Evangelism, Christian Education and Foreign Home missions.

Chi Delta Mu Fraternity f: 1913   m: 1,000
to provide a media for better communication between physicians, dentists and pharmacists.

---

f—founded
m—membership

Chi Eta Phi Sorority	f: 1932	m: 600
	to elevate nursing to a generally higher plane.	
The Drifters	f:	m: 150
	dedicated to charitable, social, civic and educational interests.	
Frontiers International	f: 1936	m: 2,000
	service to the community.	
Gamma Phi Delta Sorority	f: 1940	m:
	to encourage and finance the education and training of women in schools, colleges.	
Grand Temple Daughters I.B.P.O.E. of W.	1902	m: 150,000
	scholarship aid to deserving youth; participate in international affairs; promote financial assistance for the welfare of war orphans and health charities.	
Grand United Order of Odd Fellows	f:	m: 114,000
Improved Benevolent Protective Order of Elks of the World	f: 1898	m: 500,000
Imperial Court Daughters of Isis	f: 1910	m:
	to promote benevolent and charitable work.	
International Conference of Grand Chapters Order of the Eastern Star	f: 1907	m: 250,000
Jack and Jill	f:	m: 5,000
	to aid youth through legislation aimed at bettering conditions for all children.	
Kappa Alpha Psi Fraternity	f: 1911	m: 27,000
	to unite college men . . . to encourage honorable achievement . . . and to inspire service in the public interest.	
Knights of Peter Claver	f: 1909	m: 15,000
	to plan, promote and sponsor commendable Catholic works.	
Lambda Kappa Mu Sorority	f: 1937	m: 675
	to encourage higher education among young women.	
Links	f: 1946	m: 2,000
	interested in civic activities, intercultural relations and friendship.	
National Association for the Advancement of Colored People	f: 1909	m: 400,000
	to achieve full equality for the Negro in America.	
National Association of Barristers Wives	f: 1949	m:
	to promote a closer union and secure a more intimate relationship among the wives of lawyers, and to enhance the prestige of the legal profession.	
National Association of College Deans and Registrars	f: 1926	m: 250
	shares information of common interest regarding the administration of higher educacation and the promotion of professional welfare among its members.	

Organization	f:	m:	Purpose
National Association of College Women	1923	1500	advancement of education, civic activities and human relations.
National Association of Colored Women's Clubs		100,000	service and education
National Association of Fashion and Accessory Designers	1950	350	
National Association of Market Developers	1953	150 chapters	to raise the level of ethics and performance of those connected with the Negro market.
National Association of Ministers' Wives	1941	1,000	to foster fellowship among ministers' wives across denominational lines.
National Association of Negro Business & Prfoessional Women's Clubs	1935	25,000	to protect the interest of business and professional women and direct their attention toward united action for improved social and civic conditions.
National Association of Negro Musicians	1919	1,000	to aid young people through music scholarships, fostering professional ethics in the arts and establishing cultural institutions.
National Bankers Association	1926		to encourage the establishment and sound operation of banks by Negroes.
National Bar Association	1925	2,500	promote the legal profession.
National Beauty Culturists' League	1919	50,000	to establish more standardized and scientific methods of hair, skin and scalp treatment. Also to raise the standards of the profession.
National Business League	1900		to stimulate business and to promote the industrial, commercial and general economic welfare of Negroes.
National Conference of Artists	1959		to improve the position and promulgate the work of Negro artists in American life.
National Convention of Gospel Choirs and Choruses	1932	2,500	to elevate the standards of gospel and spiritual music.
National Council of Negro Women	1935	2,850,000	foster united planning and concerted action for the economic, social, educational and cultural welfare of Negro women.
National Dental Association	1913	1,000	
National Epicureans	1951	280	to promote the social, cultural, literary, civic and benevolent interests of its members.

National Funeral Directors and Morticians Association	f:	m: 2,000

promotes the art and science of funeral directing.

National Grand Chapter of the Eastern Star	f:	m: 10,000

auxiliary of Ancient & Accepted Scottish Rite Masons; charitable activities.

National Insurance Association	f: 1921	m: 11,000

to raise the standards and practices of the participating members.

National Medical Association	f: 1895	m: 4.200

to foster the scientific advancement of medicine.

National Newspaper Publishers Association	f: 1940	m: 50

to evaluate current trends and problems in the newspaper industry.

National Technical Association, Inc.	f: 1926	m: 300

to collect and disseminate information on existing opportunities for Negro youth in technical fields.

National United Church Ushers Association of America	f: 1919	m: 35,000

establishment of a unified system of Church ushering for all Christian churches.

National Urban League	f: 1910	m:

to eliminate segregation and discrimination in American life

Omega Psi Phi Fraternity	f: 1911	m: 10,000

fellowship, scholarship aid, social action and civil rights are foremost on its program of activities.

Phi Beta Sigma Fraternity	f: 1914	m: 12,000

social action, education and scholarship.

Tau Gamma Delta Sorority	f: 1942	m: 500

to cultivate and encourage high scholastic standards.

The Association for the Study of Negro Life and History	f: 1915	m: 2,000

to promote historical research and writing of Negro history.

MAJOR BLACK AMERICAN PUBLICATIONS

NEWSPAPERS

Alabama
Anniston. The *Mirror*, c. 2,140
Birmingham. The *Mirror*, c. 14,436
Birmingham. *Birmingham World* c. 9,700
Huntsville. The *Mirror*, c. 3,160
Mobile. Mobile *Beacon*, c. 5,500
Montgomery. Alabama *Tribune*, c. 1,500
Sheffield. *Tri-Cities Mirror*, c. 2,235
Tuscallosa. Alabama *Citizen* c. 8,000
Tuskegee. *Herald*, c. 2,740

Alaska
Anchorage. Alaska *Spotlight*, c. 1,000

Arizona
Phoenix. Arizona *Sun*, c. 5,500
Phoenix. Arizona *Tribune*, c. 3,000

Arkansas
Little Roc. Arkansas *Survey-Journal*, c. 12,550
Little Rock. Arkansas *World*, c. 13,560
Little Rock. *State Press*, c. 17,656
Pine Bluff. *Negro Spokesman*, c. 7,000

California
Los Angeles. *California Eagle*, c. 27,500
Los Angeles. *Herald-Dispatch*, c. 31,000
Los Angeles. *The Sentinel*, c. 29,810
Oakland. California *Voice*, c. 12,500
San Diego. *Comet*, c. 10,000
San Diego. *The Lighthouse*, c. 85,000
San Diego. *The Voice*, c. 12,800
San Francisco. *The Independent*, c. 8,096
San Francisco. *Sun Reporter*, c. 8,000

Colorado
Denver. *Colorado Statesman*, c. 2,900
Denver. *Star*, c. 1,200

District of Columbia
Afro-American (semi-weekly) c. 156,615 (all editions)

Florida
Jacksonville. *Florida Star-News*, c. 25,374
Jacksonville. *Florida Tattler*, c. 16,500
Miami. *Miami Times*, c. 10,500
Pensacola. *Citizen*, c. 1,100
Tampa. *Florida Sentinel-Bulletin*, c. 15,000
Tampa. *News Reporter*, c. 4,920
Sarasota. *Weekly Bulletin*, c. 4,500

Georgia
Albany. *Southwest Georgian*, c. 2,900
Atlanta. *Atlanta Daily World*, c. 29,500
Atlanta. *Atlanta Inquirer*, c. 18,911
Augusta. *Weekly Review*, c. 4,600
Voldosta. *The Telegram*, c. 10,000

Illinois
Champaign. *Illinois Times*, c. 1,500
Chicago. *Chicago Defender*, c. 31,254
Chicago. *New Crusader*, c. 19,541
East St. Louis. *The Beacon*, c. 3,500
East St. Louis. *The Crusader*, c. 7,000
Joliet. *Negro Voice*, c. 4,500
Rockford. *The Crusader*, c. 4,500

Indiana
Gary. *The American*, c. 6,885
Gary. *The Crusader*, c. 4,730
Indianapolis. *Indianapolis Recorder*, c. 11,288

111

Iowa
Des Moines. *Iowa Bystander*, c. 2,592

Kansas
Wichita. The *Enlightener*, c. 2,400

Kentucky
Louisville. *Louisville Defender*, c. 5,180

Louisiana
Baton Rouge. Baton Rouge *News Leader*, c. 9,800
Alexandria. *News Leader*, c. 10,500
Bossier City. *The Hurricane*, c. 2,375
New Orleans. *Louisiana Weekly*, c. 19,532
Shreveport. *Shreveport Sun*, c. 9,800

Maryland
Baltimore. *Afro-American*, c. 60,548

Massachusetts
Boston. *Boston Chronicle*, c. 10,509
Boston. Boston *Roxbury City News*, c. 14,000
Boston. Boston *Graphic*, c. 4,000
Boston. *The Orator*, c. 2,000
Boston. *The Times*, c. 12,000
Springfield. *The Sun*, c. 12,500

Michigan
Detroit. Michigan *Chronicle*, c. 36,639
Detroit. Michigan *Scene*, c. 4,100
Detroit. *The Tribune*, c. 28,700

Minnesota
Minneapolis. *The Spokesman*, c. 10,416
Minneapolis. *The Twin City Observer*, c. 2,000
St. Paul. *The Recorder*, c. 8,322
St. Paul. *The Sun*, c. 2,000

Mississippi
Greenville. *Delta Leader*, (Sundays) c. 3,000
Jackson. *The Jackson Advocate*, c. 4,000
Jackson. Mississippi *Free Press*, c. 8,000

Missouri
Kansas City. *Kansas City Call*, c. 21,528
St. Louis. The *American*, c. 7,200
St. Louis. The *Argus*, c. 8,761
St. Louis. *Crusader*, c. 5,000
St. Louis. *New Citizen*, c. 3,100
St. Louis. *New Crusader*, c. 4,100

Nebraska
Omaha. *Omaha Star*, c. 5,600
Omaha. *The Guide*, c. 4,050

New Jersey
Asbury Park. *Central Jersey Post*, c. 7,500
Newark, N.J. *Afro-American*, c. 5,925
Newark, N.J. *Herald News*, c. 38,080

New York
Brooklyn. N.Y. *Recorder*, c. 17,750
Buffalo. Buffalo *Empire Star*, c. 15,000
Buffalo. *Criterion*, c. 12,000
Rochester. The *American Negro*, c. 7,000
Syracuse. *Progressive World*, c. 9,300
Westchester County. Westchester County *Press*, c. 3,500
Westchester County. Westchester *Observer*, c. 7,500

New York City
N.Y. *Courier*, c. 10,932
N.Y. *Amsterdam News*, c. 89,596

North Carolina
Charlotte. *Charlotte Post*, c. 18,265
Charlotte. *Queen City Cazette*, c. 2,750
Durham. Carolina *Times*, c. 22,100
Greensboro. *Future Outlook*, c. 8,762
Raleigh. The *Carolinian*, c. 6,800
Wilmington. Wilmington *Journal*, c. 6,025

Ohio
Cincinnati. *The Herald*, c. 4,900
Cleveland. *Call & Post*, c. 27,268

Cleveland. The *Courier*, c. 10,747
Columbus. Ohio *Sentinel*, c. 3,862
Toledo. *Bronze Raven*, c. 9,500
Youngstown. *Buckeye Review*, c. 5,500

Oklahoma
Muskogee. Oklahoma *Herald*, c. 1,500
Oklahoma City. *Black Dispatch*, c. 11,688
Tulsa. Oklahoma *Eagle*, c. 6,000

Oregon
Portland. Northwest *Clarion*, c. 15,000

Pennsylvania
Philadelphia. Philadelphia *Afro-American*, c. 6,797
Philadelphia. *Courier*, c. 4,163
Philadelphia. *Independent*, c. 16,441
Philadelphia. *Tribune*, c. 50,590
Pittsburgh. Pittsburgh *Courier*, c. 15,919

Rhode Island
Providence. *Chronicle*, c. 1,541

South Carolina
Charleston. *New Citizen*, c. 2,000
Columbia. Palmetto *Times*, c. 4,000
Columbia. *Lighthouse & Informer*, c. 6,400
Greenville. *American*, c. 2,000
Kingstree. Carolina *Sun*, c. 1,000

Tennessee
Chattanooga. Chattanooga *Observer*, c. 4,500
Knoxville. *Flashlight Herald*, c. 3,700
Memphis. The *State Defender*, c. 5,648
Memphis. Memphis *World*, (semi-weekly) c. 6,000
Nashville. Nashville *Commentator*, c. 2,500

Texas
Dallas. Dallas *Express*, c. 5,045
Fort Worth. Fort Worth *Weekly*, c. 2,000
Fort Worth. Fort Worth *Mind*, c. 12,955
Houston. *Informer*, c. 15,171
Houston. Negro *Labor News* (Monthly) c. 20,000
Houston. *Sunnyside Digest*, c. 3,000
Houston. *Forward Times*, c. 12,000
San Antonio. San Antonio *Register*, c. 9,924
Waco. The *Messenger*, c. 3,400

Virginia
Charlottesville. Charlottesville-Albermarle *Tribune*, c. 2,271
Norfolk. *Journal & Guide*, c. 32,190
Richmond. Richmond *Afro-American*, c. 15,175
Roanoke. *Roanoke Tribune*, c. 15,300

West Virginia
Bluefield. *Independent Observer*, c. 2,400

Wisconsin
Milwaukee. *Gazette*, c. 11,010
Milwaukee. *The Star*, c. 6,000

NEGRO COMMERCIAL MAG. & JOURNALS

California
  Los Angeles. *American News*, c. 12,000 weekly
  Los Angeles. *Bronze America*, c. 25,000 six times per year
  Los Angeles, *Bronze California*, c. 30,000 monthly
  Los Angeles. *Elegant Magazine*, c. 60,000 bi-monthly

District of Columbia
  Journal of Negro History, c. 5,000 quarterly
  Negro History Bulletin, c. 8,900 monthly
  The Pyramid, c. 22,000

Georgia
  Atlanta. *The Foundation*, c.],500 quarterly

Illinois
  Chicago. *Ebony Magazine*, c. 825,000 quarterly
  Chicago. *Ivy Leaf*, c. 10,000 quarterly
  Chicago. *Jet Magazine*, c. 371,000 weekly
  Chicago. *Tan Magazine*, c. 123,000 monthly

New York
  Bronx. *On the Ball Magazine*, c. 5,000 quarterly
  New York. *African Heritage*, c. 15,000 monthly
  New York. *African Opinion*, c. 3,000 bi-monthly
  New York. *Freedom Ways*, c. 5,000 quarterly
  New York. *Journal of the National Medical Association*, c. 3,600 bi-monthly
  New York. *Link Magazine*, monthly
  New York. *News Illustrated*, c. 4,000 monthly
  New York. *The Voice*, c. 50,000 monthly
  New York. *Voice of Missions*, c. 10,000 monthly

Ohio
  Wilberforce. *Index to Selected Periodicals*, c. 1,000 quarterly
  Wilberforce. *Journal of Human Relations*, c. 1,200 quarterly

Tennessee
  Nashville. *Kappa Alpha Psi Journal*, c. 3,000 quarterly

Texas
  Fort Worth. *Bronze Thrills, Hep, Jive, Sepia*, c. 400,000 combined

RELIGIOUS PUBLICATIONS

Alabama
  Birmingham. *Baptist Leader*, c. 2,112 weekly
  Tuskegee. *Campus Digest*, c. 3,000 bi-weekly

District of Columbia
  Journal of Religious Thought, c. 1,500 semi-annual

Georgia
  Atlanta. *The Center*, c. 1,500 quarterly

Mississippi
  Bay St. Louis. *St. Augustine's Messenger*, c. 5,000 monthly

North Carolina
  Charlotte. *Star of Zion*, c. 4,500 weekly

Pennsylvania
  Philadelphia. *AME Church Review*, c. 5,000 quarterly

Tennessee
  Jackson. *Christian Index*, c. 5,000 weekly
  Nashville. *The Message Magazine*, c. 50,000 weekly
  Nashville. *The Review*, c. 2,000 monthly
  Nashville. *Union Review*, c. 5,000 weekly

COLLEGIATE PUBLICATIONS

Hornet & Freshmore	Alabama State College (Montgomery, Alabama)	c. 2,000 bi-monthly
The Hornet	State Teachers College (Dover, Delaware)	c. 1,500 bi-monthly
Howard University Magazine	Howard University (Washington, D.C.)	c. 7,500
Atlanta University Bulletin	Atlanta University (Atlanta, Georgia)	c. 3,500 quarterly
The Maroon Tiger	Morehouse College (Atlanta, Georgia)	c. 2,500 bi-monthly
Phylon	Atlanta University (Atlanta, Georgia)	c. 2,500 quarterly
The Digest	Southern University (Baton Rouge, Louisiana)	c. 4,000 bi-weekly
CLA Journal	College Language Association (Baltimore, Maryland)	c. 600 (three times yearly)
Quarterly Review of Higher Education	Durham, North Carolina	c. 1,000 quarterly
The Register	A. & T. College (Greensboro, North Carolina)	c. 3,000 monthly
The Gold Torch	Central State College (Wilberforce, Ohio)	c. 2,500 bi-monthly
The Broadcaster	A. & I. State university (Nashville, Tennessee)	c. 5,000 monthly
The Herald	Texas Southern University (Houston, Texas)	c. 3,500 monthly
Hampton Script	Hampton Institute (Hampton, Virginia)	c. 2,000 bi-monthly
Virginia Statesman	Virginia State College (Petersburg, Virginia)	c. 1,500 weekly
The Bluefieldian	West Virginia State College (Bluefield, West Virginia)	c. 2,000 monthly

MUSEUMS AND MONUMENTS
OF
AFRO-AMERICAN INTEREST

NEGROES

Tuskegee Institute, George Washington Carver Museum (founded 1938), P.O. Box 40, Tuskegee, Ala. Mon.-Sat., 10-4; Sun., 1-4; closed holidays. Admission free.

George Washington Carver National Monument (founded 1952), P.O. Box 38, Diamond, Mo. Daily, 8:30-5; closed Christmas. Admission free.

Dunbar House, 219 Summit St., Dayton, Ohio. June-Sept. 15, weekends and holidays, 10-5; school groups by appointment, April-Sept. Admission: adults, 15 cents; children, 10 cents.

Chatham-Kent Museum (founded 1943; opened 1945), 59 William St. North, Chatham, Ontario, Canada. Tues., Thurs., Sat., 3-5, 7:30-9; first and third Sun., 3-5. Admission: adults, 25 cents; children, 10 cents; children accompanied by adults, free; group rates.

"Uncle Tom's Cabin" (founded 1948), Dresden, Ontario, Canada. April-Nov., daily, 10-sunset. Admission: adults, 50 cents; children, 10 cents; group rates.

Wilberforce University, Carnegie Library (founded 1953), Wilberforce, Ohio. Mon., Tues., Thurs., Fri., 9-4; Wed., 9-11, 1-4; Sat., 9-12; Sun., 5-7:30; Mon.-Fri. eves., 6-9. Admission free.

NEGRO ART AND MUSIC

Howard University Gallery of Art (founded 1930), College of Fine Arts, 2455 Sixth St., N.W., Box 1023 (1), Washington, D.C. Mon.-Fri., 9-5; Sat., 10-12; closed holidays. Admission free.

Museum of Negro History and Art, Chicago, Ill.

New Orleans Jazz Museum (founded 1961), 1017 Dumaine St., New Orleans, La. Tues.-Sat. and holidays, 10-5; Sun., 1-5; closed Christmas. Admission: 25 cents.

NEGRO HISTORY

American Society of African Culture, 15 East 40th St., New York City.

Association for the Study of Negro Life and History (founded 1915), 1538 Ninth St., N.W., Washington, D.C. 20001. Mon.-Fri., 8:30-5.

Soper Collection, Morgan State College, Baltimore, Md.

Stowe House, 2950 Gilbert Ave., Cincinnati, Ohio. June-Sept. 15, weekends and holidays, 9:30-5; school groups by appointment, April-Sept. Admission: adults, 15 cents; children 10 cents; school groups with teacher, free.

Harriet Beecher Stowe House, 73 Forest St., Hartford, Conn. Not open to the public.

The Old Slave Mart (founded 1938), 6 Chalmers St., Charleston, S.C. 29401. Mon.-Sat., 10-5 (winter); summer schedule varies; closed national holidays. Admission: museum, adults, 50 cents; children 6-12, 25 cents; art gallery, free.

SLAVERY

Stratford Historical Society (founded 1925), 967 Academy Hill, Stratford, Conn. Wed., Sat., Sun., 11-5 (May-Labor Day); Thurs., Fri., Sat., 1-5 (Labor Day-May 1); and by appointment. Admission: adults, 75 cents; children, 20 cents.

Wallace House (opened 1897), 38 Washington Place, Somerville, N.J. Tues.-Sat., 10-12. 1-5; Sun., holidays, 2-5; closed Thanksgiving, Christmas, New Year's. Admission: adults, 25 cents; children 5-12, 10 cents; school groups free.

Zebulon B. Vance Birthplace (founded 1959; open 1961), Reems Creek Road, Weaverville, N.C. Tues.-Fri., 9-5; Sat., Sun., 2-5 (April-Oct.); Wed., 9-5; Sun., 2-5 (Nov.-March); closed Thanksgiving, Christmas, New Year's. Admission: adults, 25 cents; children, 10 cents.

Sam Davis Memorial Association (founded 1927; opened 1930), Smyrna, Tenn. Mon.-Sat., 8-5; Sun., 1-5; closed Thanksgiving, Christmas. Admission: adults, 50 cents; children, 25 cents; group rates.

Colonel E. S. Robertson Home, U.S. Highway 81, Salado, Tex. Mar. 15-June 15, Sept. 15-Oct. 15, Mon.-Sat., 10-5; Sun., 1:30-5; closed holidays. Admission: adults, 75 cents; children, 60 cents.

University of Virginia, Orland E. White Research Arboretum (founded 1928), Boyce, Va. By appointment. Admission free.

Booker T. Washington National Monument (founded 1957; opened 1963), Virginia Route 122, 16 mi. N.E. of Rocky Mount, Va. Daily, 8-5; closed Christmas. Admission free.

Fort Malden National Historic Park (founded 1941), 312 Laird Ave., Amherstburg, Ontario, Canada. Mon.-Sat., 9-8; Sun., 12-8 (July, Aug.); Mon.-Sat., 9-5; Sun., 1-5 (May, June, Sept.); Mon.-Sat., 10-4:30; Sun., 1-4:40 (Oct.-Apr.); closed New Year's, Good Friday, Christmas. Admission free.

ABOLITION

Commodore Perry Memorial House and Dickson Tavern (opened 1963), 201 French St., Erie, Penna. Sat., Sun., 1-4; June 15-Sept. 15, daily 1-4. Admission: adults, 25 cents; children, 10 cents.

Rowland E. robinson Memorial Association (founded 1937; opened 1963), Ferrisburg, Vt. June-Sept., daily, 8-8.

Lincoln-Tallman Museum (founded 1951), 440 North Jackson St., Janesville, Wisc. May 15-Oct., Mon.-Sat., 9-5; Sun., 11-5. Admission: adults, 50 cents; 'children 12-18, 35 cents; under 12, 15 cents.

SELECTED QUOTATIONS

1688. *Quakers of Germantown, Pennsylvania, made the first formal protest against slavery in the Western Hemisphere.* February 11.

. . . There is a saying, that we should do to all men like as we will be done for ourselves. . . . Here [in America] is liberty of conscience, which is right and reasonable; here ought to be likewise liberty of the body. . . . But to bring men hither, or to rob and sell them against their will, we stand against. . . . Pray, what thing in the world can be done worse towards us, that if men should rob or steal us away, and sell us for slaves to strange countries; separating husbands from their wives and children. . . .

. . . have these poor Negroes not as much right to fight for their freedom, as you have to keep them slaves?

George H. Moore, *Notes on the History of Slavery in Massachusetts* (New York, 1866), pp. 75-77.

1776. *Phillis Wheatley was invited by General Washington to visit him at his headquarters in Cambridge, Massachusetts, so that he might express appreciation for her poem in his honor.* February 28.

Miss. Phillis: Your favour of the 26th of October did not reach my hands 'till the middle of December. Time enough, you will say, to have given an answer ere this. Granted. . . .

I thank you most sincerely for your polite notice of me, in the elegant lines you enclosed; and however undeserving I may be of such encomium and panegyrick, the style and manner exhibit a striking proof of your great poetical Talents. In honour of which, and in a tribute justly due you, I would have published the Poem, had I not been apprehensive, that, while I only meant to give the World this new instance of your genius, I might have incurred the imputation of Vanity. This and nothing else, determined me not to give it place in the public prints.

If you should ever come to Cambridge, or near Head Quarters, I shall be happy to see a person so favoured by the Muses, and to whom Nature has been so liberal and beneficient in her dispensations. I am, with great Respect, etc.

John C. Fitzpatrick, ed., *The Writings of George Washington from the Original Manuscript Sources 1754-1799*, Vol. 4 (Washington, 1938), p. 360.

1814. *General Andrew Jackson appealed to free Negroes to fight as part of the militia.* September 21.

PROCLAMATION
To the free colored inhabitants of Louisiana

Through a mistaken policy you have heretofore been deprived of a participation in the glorious struggle for national rights in which our country is engaged. This no longer shall exist.

As sons of freedom, you are now called upon to defend our most inestimable blessing. As Americans, you country looks with confidence to her adopted children, for a valorous support, as a faithful return for the advantages enjoyed under her mild and equitable government. As fathers, husbands, and brothers, you are summoned to rally round the standard of the Eagle, to defend all which is dear in existence.

Your country, although calling for your exertions, does not wish yo to engage in her cause, without amply remunerating you for the services rendered. Your intelligent minds are not to be led away by false representations.—Your love of honor would cause you to despise the man who should attempt to deceive you. In the sincerity of a soldier, and the language of truth I address you.

SELECTED QUOTATIONS

To every noble hearted, generous, freeman of color, volunteering to serve during the present contest with Great Britain, and no longer, there will be paid the same bounty in money and lands, now received by the white soldiers of the U. States, viz. one hundred and twenty-four dollars in money, and one hundred and sixty acres of land. The non-commissioned officers and privates will also be entitled to the same monthly pay and daily rations, and clothes furnished to any American soldier.

On enrolling yourselves in companies, the major-general commanding will select officers for your government, from your white fellow citizens. Your non-commissioned officers will be appointed from among yourselves.

Due regard will be paid to the feelings of freemen and soldiers. You will not, by being associated with white men in the same corps, be exposed to improper comparisons or unjust sarcasm. As a distinct, independent battalion or regiment, pursuing the path of glory, you will, undivided, receive the applause and gratitude of your countrymen.

To assure you of the sincerity of my intentions and my anxiety to engage your invaluable services to our country, I have communicated my wishes to the governor of Louisiana, who is fully informed as to the manner of enrollment, and will give you every necessary information on the subject of this address.

Headquarters, 7th military district,
Mobile, Sept. 21st 1814
Andrew Jackson,
Maj. gen, commanding
Niles' Weekly Register, Vol. 7, Dec. 3, 1814.

1817 *James Forten, Negro abolitionist, was chairman of the First Negro Convention held in Philadelphia.* January 23.

Esteemed friend. . . .

The African Institution met at the Rev. R. Allens the very night your letter came to hand. I red that part to them that wished them a happy New Year, for which they desired me to return you many thanks. I must now mention to you that the whole continent seems to be agitated concerning Colonising the People of Colour. . . . Indeed the People of Colour, here was very much fritened at first. They were afrade that all the free people would be Compelled to go, particularly in the southern States. We had a large meeting of Males at the Rev. R. Allens Church the other evening. Three thousand at least attended, and there was not one sole that was in favour of going to Africa. They think that the slave holders want to get rid of them so as to make their property more secure. However it appears to me that if the Father of all mercies, is in this interesting subject . . . the way will be made strate and clear. We however have agreed to remain silent, as the people here both the white & colour are decided against the measure. My opinion is that they will never become a people until they come out from amongst the white people, but as the majority is decidedly against me I am determined to remain silent, accept as to my opinion which I freely give when asked. . . .

I remain very affectionately
Yours unalterably,
James Forten
James Forten, *Letter of January 25, 1817,
in Paul Cuffe Papers* (New Bedford Library)

1829   *"Walker's Appeal," militant anti-slavery pamphlet published by David Walker, was distributed throughout the country and aroused the Negroes and provoked slave-holders.* January 18.

. . . Remember, Americans, that we must and shall be free and enlightened as you are, will you wait until we shall, under God, obtain our liberty, by the crushing arm of power? Will it not be dreadful for you? I speak Americans for your good. We must and shall be free I say, in spite of you. You may do your best to keep us in wretchedness and misery, to enrich you and your children, but God will deliver us from under you. And wo, wo, will be to you if we have to obtain our freedom by fighting. Throw away your fears and prejudices then, and enlighten us and treat us like men, and we will like you more than we do now hate you, and tell us no more about colonization (to Africa), for America is as much our country, as it is yours.—Treat us like men, and there is no danger but we will all live in peace and happiness together. For we are not like you, hard hearted, unmerciful, and unforgiving. What a happy country this will be, if the whites will listen. . . . But Americans, I declare to you, while you keep us and our children in bondage, and treat us like brutes, to make us support you and your families, we cannot be your friends. You do not look for it, do you? Treat us then like men, and we will be your friends. . . .

David Walker, *Walker's Appeal, in Four Articles* (Boston, 1830), pp. 79-80.

1843   *Henry Highland Garnet made controversial speech at the National Convention of Colored Men in Buffalo calling for a slave revolt and a general strike.* August 22.

Brethren, it is as wrong for your lordly oppressors to keep you in slavery as it was for the man thief to steal our ancestors from the coast of Africa. You should therefore now use the same manner of resistance as would have been just in our ancestors when the bloody foot prints of the first remorseless soul-thief was placed upon the shores of our fatherland. . . .

Brethren, the time has come when you must act for yourselves. It is an old and true saying, "if hereditary bondsmen would be free, they must themselves strike the blow." You can plead your own cause, and do the work of emancipation better than any others. . . . Think of the undying glory that hangs around the ancient name of Africa—and forget not that you are native-born American citizens, and as such, you are justly entitled to all the rights that are granted to the freest. Think how many tears you have poured out upon the soil which you have cultivated with unrequited toil and enriched with your blood; and then go to your lordly enslavers and tell them plainly, that *you are determined to be free.* Appeal to their sense of justice, and tell them that they have no more right to oppress you than you have to enslave them. . . . Inform them that all you desire is FREEDOM and that nothing else will suffice. Do this, and forever after cease to toil for the heartless tyrants, who give you no other reward but stripes and abuse. If they then commence worth of death, they, and not you, will be responsible for the consequences. You had better far all die—*die immediately,* then live slaves, and entail your wretchedness upon your posterity. If you would be free in this generation, here is your only hope. However much you and all of us may desire it, there is not much hope of redemption without the shedding of blood. If you must bleed, let it all come at once—rather *die freemen than to live to be slaves.* . . .

SELECTED QUOTATIONS

Brethren, arise, arise! Strike for your lives and liberties. Now is the day and the hour. Let every slave throughout the land do this, and the days of slavery are numbered. You cannot be more oppressed than you have been—you cannot suffer greater cruelties than you have already. *Rather die freemen than live to be slaves.* Remember that you are FOUR MILLIONS!

A Memorial Discourse by Rev. Henry Highland Garnet, James M. Smith, ed. (Philadelphia, 1865), pp. 48-59.

1862 *Charlotte Forten, Negro poet and teacher, arrived in St. Helena, South Carolina, to teach Negroes.* October 29.

... I never before saw children so eager to learn, although I have had several years' experience in New-England schools. Coming to school is a constant delight and recreation to them. They come here as other children go to play. The older ones, during the summer, work in the fields from early morning until eleven or twelve o'clock, and then come to school, after their hard toil in the hot sun, as bright and as anxious to learn as ever. ...

Charlotte Forten, "Life on the Sea Islands," *Atlantic Monthly,* XIII (March, 1864), p. 591.

1864 *In a duel between USS Kearsage and CSS Alabama off the coast of France, a Negro sailor, Joachim Pease, displayed "marked coolness," and won the Congressional Medal of Honor.* June 19.

{Joachim Pease, Seaman} served as seaman on board the U.S.S. *Kearsage* when she destroyed the *Alabama* off Cherbourg, France, 19 June 1864. Acting as loader during this bitter engagement, PEASE exhibited marked coolness and good conduct and was highly recommended by his divisional officer for gallantry under fire. General Order 45, Dec. 31, 1864.

The United States Navy, *Medal of Honor, 1861-1949,* p. 43.

1868 *Fourteenth Amendment became part of the Constitution.* July 28.

No State shall make or enforce any law which shall abridge the privileges or immunities of citizens of the United States, nor shall any State deprive any person of life, liberty, or property without due process of law; nor deny to any person within its jurisdiction the equal protection of the laws.

Amendment 14, Section 1 (1868).

1872 *P.B.S. Pinchback became Acting Governor of Louisiana on the impeachment of the Governor.* December 11.

... several Senators (I hope they are not Republicans) think me a very bad man. If this be true I fear my case is hopeless, for I am a bad man in the eyes of the democracy {and} weak-kneed Republicans. But of what does my badness consist? I am bad because I have dared on several important occasions to have an independent opinion. I am bad because I have dared at all times to advocate and insist on exact and equal justice to all Mankind. I am bad because having colored blood in my veins I have dared to aspire to the United States Senate, and I am bad because your representatives dared express the will of the people rather than obey the will of those who thought they were the peoples' Masters, when they elected me.

Friends I have been told that if I dared utter such Sentiments as these in public that I certainly would be Kept out of the Senate, all I have to say in answer to this, is that if I cannot enter the Senate except with bated breath and on bended knees, I prefer not to enter at all. ...

P.B.S. Pinchback, *Pinchback's Handwritten Manuscript: Notes for a Speech,* from Howard University's Moorland Collection (Washington, 1873).

1895   *Booker T. Washington delivered his famous "Atlanta Compromise" address at Cotton Exposition in Atlanta, Georgia.* September 18.

. . . To those of my race who depend on bettering their condition in a foreign land or who underestimate the importance of cultivating friendly relations with the Southern white man, who is their next-door neighbor, I would say: "Cast down your bucket where you are"—cast it down in making friends in every manly way, of the people of all races by whom you are surrounded.

Cast it down in agriculture, mechanics, in commerce, in domestic service, and in the professions. . . . Our greatest danger is that in the great leap from slavery to freedom we may overlook the fact that the masses of us are to live by the productions of our hands, and fail to keep in mind that we shall prosper in proportion as we learn to dignify and glorify common labour and put brains and skill into the common occupations of life; shall prosper in proportion as we learn to draw the line between the superficial and the substantial, the ornamental gewgaws of life and the useful. No race can prosper till it learns that there is as much dignity in tilling a field as in writing a poem. It is at the bottom of life we must begin, and not at the top. Nor should we permit our grievances to overshadow our opportunities.

To those of the white race . . . were I permitted I would repeat what I say to my own race: "Cast down your bucket where you are." Cast it down among the eight millions of Negroes whose habits you know, whose fidelity and love you have tested in day when to have proved treacherous meant the ruin of your firesides. Cast down your bucket among these people who have, without strikes and labour wars, tilled your fields, cleared your forests, builded your railroads and cities, and brought forth treasures from the bowels of the earth. . . . Casting down your bucket among my people, helping and encouraging them as you are doing on these grounds, and to education of head, hand, and heart, you will find that they will buy your surplus land, make blossom the waste places in your fields, and run your factories. While doing this, you can be sure in the future, as in the past, that you and your families will be surrounded by the most patient, faithful, law-abiding, and unresentful people that the world has seen. As we have proved our loyalty to you in the past, in nursing your children, watching by the sick-bed of your mothers and fathers and often following them with tear-dimmed eyes to their graves so in the future, in our humble way, we shall stand by you with a devotion that no foreigner can approach, ready to lay down our lives, if need be, in defence of yours, interlacing our industrial, commercial, civil, and religious life with yours in a way that shall make the interests of both races one. In all things that are purely social we can be as separate as the fingers, yet one as the had in all things essential to mutual progress.

There is no defence or security for any of us except in the highest intelligence and development of all. If anywhere there are efforts tending to curtail the fullest growth of the Negro, let these efforts be turned to stimulating, encouraging, and making him the most useful and intelligent citizen. Effort or means so invested will pay a thousand per cent interest. These efforts will be twice blessed—"blessing him that gives and him that takes.". . .

Nearly sixteen millions of hands will aid you in pulling the load upward, or they will pull against you the load downward. We shall constitute one-third and more of the ignorance and crime of the South, or one-third its intelligence and progress; we shall contribute one-third to the business and industrial prosperity of the South, or we shall prove a veritable body of death, stagnating, depressing, retarding every effort to advance the body politic . . . .

The wisest among my race understand that the agitation of questions of social equality is the extremest folly, and that progress in the enjoyment of all the privileges that will come to us must be the result of severe and constant struggle rather than of artificial forcing. No race that has anything to contribute to the markets of the world is long in any degree ostracized. It is important and right that all privileges of the law be ours, but it is vastly more important that we be prepared for the exercises of these privileges. The opportunity to earn a dollar in a factory just now is worth infinitely more than the opportunity to spend a dollar in an opera house.

. . . I pledge that in your effort to work out the great and intricate problem which God has laid at the doors of the South, you shall have at all times the patient, sympathetic help of my race. . . .

Booker T. Washington, *Up From Slavery* (New York, 1901), pp. 218-225.

1895 Ida B. Wells compiled the first statistical pamphlet on lynching, *The Red Record*.

. . . We demand a fair trial by law for those accused of crime, and punishment by law after honest conviction. No maudlin sympathy for criminals is solicited, but we do ask that the law shall punish all alike. We earnestly desire those that control the forces which make public sentiment to join with us in the demand. Surely the humanitarian spirit of this country which reaches out to denounce the treatment of Russian Jews, the Armenian Christians, the laboring poor of Europe, the Siberian exiles, and the native women of India—will not longer refuse to lift its voice on this subject. If it were known that the cannibals or the savage Indians had burned three human beings alive in the past two years, the whole of Christendom would be aroused, to devise ways and means to put a stop to it. Can you remain silent and inactive when such things are done in our own community and country? Is your duty to humanity in the United States less binding?

Ida B. Wells, *A Red Record* (Chicago, 1894), p. 97.

1896 United States Supreme Court decision of Plessy v. Ferguson *upheld doctrine of "separate but equal."* May 18.

This case turns upon the constitutionality of an act of the General Assembly of the State of Louisiana, passed in 1890, providing for separate carriages for the white and colored races. . . .

The first section of the statute enacts "that all railway companies carrying passengers in their coaches in this State, shall provide equal but separate accommodations for the white and colored races. . . .

The object of the [Fourteenth] Amendment was undoubtedly to enforce the absolute equality of the two races before the law, but in the nature of things it could not have been intended to abolish distinctions based upon color, or to enforce social, as distinguished from political equality, or a commingling of the two races upon terms unsatisfactory to either. Laws permitting, and even requiring, their separation in places where they are liable to be brought into contact do not necessarily imply the inferiority of either race to the other, and have been generally, if not universally, recognized as within the competency of the state legislatures in the exercise of their police power. The most common instance of this is connected with the establishment of separate schools for white and colored children, which has been held to be a valid exercise of the legislative power even by courts of States where the political rights of the colored race have been longest and most earnestly enforced. . . .

We consider the underlying fallacy of the plaintiff's argument to consist in the assumption that the enforced separation of the two races stamp the colored race with a badge of inferiority. If this be so, it is not by reason of anything found in the act, but solely because the colored race chooses to put that construction upon it. . . . The argument also assumes that social prejudices may be overcome by legislation, and that equal rights cannot be secured to the Negro except by an enforced commingling of the two races. We cannot accept this proposition. If the two races are to meet upon terms of social equality, it must be the result of natural affinities, a mutual appreciation of each other's merits and a voluntary consent of individuals. . . . Legislation is powerless to eradicate racial instincts or to abolish distinctions based upon physical differences, and the attempt to do so can only result in accentuating the difficulties of the present situation. If the civil and political rights of both races be equal, one cannot be inferior to the other civilly or politically. If one race be inferior to the other socially, the Constitution of the United States cannot put them upon the same plane.
163 U.S. 537 (1896).

1903   *W.E.B. DuBois published his* Souls of Black Folk.
. . . in the history of nearly all other races and peoples the doctrine preached . . . has been that manly self-respect is worth more than land and houses, and that a people who voluntarily surrender such respect, or cease striving for it, are not worth civilizing.

In answer to this, it has been claimed that the Negro can survive only through submission. Mr. Washington distinctly asks that black people give up, at least for the present, three things,—

First, political power,

Second, insistence on civil rights,

Third, higher education of Negro youth,—

and concentrate all their energies on industrial education, the accumulation of wealth, and the conciliation of the South. . . . As a result of this tender of the palm-branch, what has been the return? In these years {since Booker T. Washington's Atlanta address} there have occurred:

1. The disfranchisement of the Negro.
2. The legal creation of a distinct status of civil inferiority.
3. The steady withdrawal of aid from institutions for the higher training of the Negro.

These movements are not, to be sure, direct results of Mr. Washington's teachings; but his propaganda has, without a shadow of a doubt, helped their speedier accomplishment. . . .

{Negroes} do not expect that the free right to vote, to enjoy civic rights, and to be educated, will come in a moment, they do not expect to see the biases and prejudices of years disappear at the blast of a trumpet; but they are absolutely certain that the way for a people to gain their reasonable rights is not by voluntarily throwing them away and insisting that they do not want them; that the way for a people to gain respect is not by continually belittling and ridiculing themselves; that on the contrary, Negroes must insist continually, in season and out of season, that voting is necessary to proper manhood, that color discrimination is barbarism, and that black boys need education as well as white boys. . . .
W. E. Du Bois, The Souls of Black Folk
(Chicago, 1903), pp. 51-59.

1906 *Paul Laurence Dunbar, the poet, died in Dayton, Ohio.* February 9.

"We Wear The Mask"

We wear the mask that grins and lies,
It hides our cheeks and shades our eyes,—
This debt we pay to human guile;
With torn and bleeding hearts we smile,
And mouth with myriad subtleties.

Why should the world be over-wise,
In counting all our tears and sighs?
Nay, let them only see us, while
    We wear the mask.

We smile, but, O great Christ, our cries
To thee from tortured souls arise.
We sing, but oh the clay is vile
Beneath our feet, and long the mile;
But let the world dream otherwise,
    We wear the mask!

Paul Laurence Dunbar, *Lyrics of Lowly Life* (New York, 1899), p. 167.

1956 *Manifesto denouncing U.S. Supreme Court ruling on segregation in public schools was issued by one hundred Southern Senators and Representatives.* March 11.

We regard the decision of the Supreme Court in the school cases as a clear abuse of judicial power. It climaxes a trend in the federal judiciary undertaking to legislate, in derogation of the authority of Congress, and to encroach upon the reserved rights of the states and the people.

The Original Constitution does not mention education. Neither does the Fourteenth Amendment or any other amendment. The debates preceding the submission of the Fourteenth Amendment clearly show that there was no intent that it should affect the systems of education maintained by the states. . . .

In the case of *Plessy v. Ferguson* in 1896 the Supreme Court expressly declared that under the Fourteenth Amendment no person was denied any of his rights if the states provided separate but equal public facilities. This decision has been followed in many other cases. . . .

This interpretation, restated time and again, became a part of the life of the people of many of the states and confirmed their habits, customs, tradition, and way of life. It is founded on elemental humanity and common sense, for parents should not be deprived by government of the right to direct the lives and education of their own children.

. . . the Supreme Court of the United States, with no legal basis for such action, undertook to exercise their naked judicial power and substituted their personal political and social ideas for the established law of the land.

This unwarranted exercise of power by the Court, . . . is destroying the amicable relations between the white and Negro races that have been created through 90 years of patient effort by the good people of both races. It has planted hatred and suspicion where heretofore there has been friendship and understanding.

Without regard to the consent of the governed, outside agitators are threatening immediate and revolutionary changes in our public school systems. If done, this is certain to destroy the system of public education in some of the states.

New York Times, March 12, 1956, p. 19.

1963 *President Kennedy said nation faced "moral crisis" over Negro demands for equality; pledged legislation to open public facilities for all (TV address).* June 12.

. . . This Nation was founded by men of many nations and backgrounds. It was founded on the principle that all men are created equal, and that the rights of every man are diminished when the rights of one man are threatened.

Today we are committed to a worldwide struggle to promote and protect the rights of all who wish to be free. And when Americans are sent to Vietnam or West Berlin, we do not ask for whites only. It ought to be possible, therefore, for American students of any color to attend any public institution they select without having to be backed up by troops.

It ought to be possible for American consumers of any color to receive equal service in places of public accommodation, such as hotels and restaurants and theatres and retail stores, without being forced to resort to demonstrations in the street, and it ought to be possible for American citizens of any color to register and to vote in a free election without interference or fear of reprisal.

It ought to be possible, in short, for every American to enjoy the privileges of being American without regard to his race or his color. In short, every American ought to have the right to be treated as he would wish to be treated, as one would wish his children to be treated. But this is not the case.

The Negro baby born in America today, regardless of the section of the nation in which he is born, has about one-half as much chance of completing a high school education as a white baby born in the same place on the same day, one-third as much chance of completing college, one-third as much chance of becoming a professional man, twice as much chance of becoming unemployed, about one-seventh as much chance of earning $10,000 a year, a life expectancy which is 7 years shorter, and the prospects of earning only half as much.

This is not a sectional issue. Difficulties over segregation and discrimination exist in every city, in every State of the Union, producing in many cities a rising tide of discontent that threatens the public safety. Nor is this a partisan issue.

In a time of domestic crisis men of good will and generosity should be able to unite regardless of party or politics. This is not even a legal or legislative issue alone. It is better to settle these matters in the courts than on the streets, and new laws are needed at every level, but law alone cannot make men see right.

We are confronted primarily with a moral issue. It is as old as the scriptures and is as clear as the American Constitution.

The heart of the question is whether all Americans are to be afforded equal rights and equal opportunities, whether we are going to treat our fellow Americans as we want to be treated. If an American, because his skin is dark, cannot eat lunch in a restaurant open to the public, if he cannot send his children to the best public school available, if he cannot vote for the public officials who represent him, if, in short, he cannot enjoy the full and free life which all of us want, then who among us would be content to have the color of his skin changed and stand in his place? Who among us would then be content with the counsels of patience and delay?

One hundred years of delay have passed since President Lincoln freed the slaves, yet their heirs, their grandsons, are not fully free. They are not yet freed from the bonds of injustice. They are not yet freed from social and economic oppression. And this Nation, for all its hopes and all its boasts, will not be fully free until all its citizens are free.

We preach freedom around the world, and we mean it, and we cherish our freedom here at home, but are we to say to the world, and much more importantly, to each other that this is a land of the free except for the Negroes;

that we have no second-class citizens except Negroes; that we have no class or caste system, no ghettoes, no master race except with respect to Negroes?

Now the time has come for this Nation to fulfill its promise. The events in Birmingham and elsewhere have so increased the cries for equality that no city or State or legislative body can prudently choose to ignore them.

The fires of frustration and discord are burning in every city, North and South, where legal remedies are not at hand. Redress is sought in the streets, in demonstrations, parades, and protests which create tensions and threaten violence and threaten lives.

We face, therefore, a moral crisis as a country and as a people. It cannot be met by repressive police action. It cannot be left to increased demonstrations in the streets. It cannot be quieted by token moves or talk. It is a time to act in the Congress, in your State and local legislative body and, above all, in all of our daily lives.

It is not enough to pin the blame on others, to say this is a problem of one section of the country or another, or deplore it. A great change is at hand, and our task, our obligation, is to make that revolution, that change, peaceful and constructive for all.

Those who do nothing are inviting shame as well as violence. Those who act boldly are recognizing right as well as reality.

Next week I shall ask the Congress of the United States to act, to make a commitment it has not fully made in this century to the proposition that race has no place in American life or law. . . .

John F. Kennedy, *Public Papers of the Presidents of the United States,* Vol. III (Washington, 1964), pp. 236-237.

BLACK MEMBERS OF THE CONGRESS OF THE UNITED STATES

41st Congress, 1869-71

Joseph Hayne Rainey, South Carolina
Jefferson F. Long, Georgia
Hiram Rhodes Revels, Mississippi*

42nd Congress, 1871-73

Josiah Thomas Walls, Florida
Benjamin Sterling Turner, Alabama
Joseph Hayne Rainey, South Carolina
Robert Brown Eliott, South Carolina

43rd Congress, 1873-75

Robert Brown Eliott, South Carolina
Richard Harvey Cain, South Carolina
Alonzo Jacob Ransier, South Carolina
James Thomas Rapier, Alabama
Josiah Thomas Walls, Florida
John R. Lynch, Mississippi

44th Congress, 1875-77

John R. Lynch, Mississippi
Blanche K. Bruce, Mississippi*
Josiah Thomas Walls, Florida
Jeremiah Haralson, Alabama
John Adams Hyman, North Carolina
Charles Edmund Nash, Louisiana
Robert Smalls, South Carolina

45th Congress, 1877-79

Richard Harvey Cain, South Carolina
Joseph Hayne Rainey, South Carolina
Robert Smalls, South Carolina
Blanche K. Bruce, Mississippi*

46th Congress, 1879-81

Blanche K. Bruce, Mississippi*

47th Congress, 1881-83

Robert Smalls, South Carolina

48th Congress, 1883-85

Robert Smalls, South Carolina
James O'Hara, North Carolina

49th Congress, 1885-87

Robert Smalls, South Carolina
James O'Hara, North Carolina

51st Congress, 1889-91

Henry Plummer Cheatham, North Carolina
Thomas Ezekiel Miller, South Carolina
John Mercer Langston, Virginia

52nd Congress, 1891-93

Henry P. Cheatham, North Carolina

53rd Congress, 1893-95

George Washington Murray, South Carolina

54th Congress, 1895-99

George Washington Murray, South Carolina

55th Congress, 1897-99

George H. White, North Carolina

* Served in Senate, all others House of Representatives

MEMBERS OF THE CONGRESS

56th Congress, 1899-01

George H. White, North Carolina

72nd Congress, 1931-33

Oscar DePriest, Illinois

73rd Congress, 1933-35

Oscar DePriest, Illinois

74th Congress, 1935-37

Arthur W. Mitchell, Illinois

75th Congress, 1937-39

Arthur W. Mitchell, Illinois

76th Congress, 1939-41

Arthur W. Mitchell, Illinois

77th Congress, 1941-43

Arthur W. Mitchell, Illinois

78th Congress, 1943-45

William L. Dawson, Illinois

79th Congress, 1945-47

William L. Dawson, Illinois
Adam Clayton Powell, Jr., New York

80th Congress, 1947-49

William L. Dawson, Illinois
Adam Clayton Powell, Jr., New York

81st Congress, 1949-51

William L. Dawson, Illinois
Adam Clayton Powell, Jr., New York

82nd Congress, 1951-53

William L. Dawson, Illinois
Adam Clayton Powell, Jr., New York

83rd Congress, 1953-55

William L. Dawson, Illinois
Adam Clayton Powell, Jr., New York

84th Congress, 1955-57

William L. Dawson, Illinois
Adam Clayton Powell, Jr., New York
Charles C. Diggs, Michigan

85th Congress, 1957-59

William L. Dawson, Illinois
Adam Clayton Powell, Jr., New York
Charles C. Diggs, Michigan

86th Congress, 1959-61

William L. Dawson, Illinois
Adam Clayton Powell, Jr., New York
Charles C. Diggs, Michigan
Robert N.C. Nix, Pennsylvania

87th Congress, 1961-63

William L. Dawson, Illinois
Adam Clayton Powell, Jr., New York
Charles C. Diggs, Michigan
Robert N.C. Nix, Pennsylvania

88th Congress, 1963-65

William L. Dawson, Illinois
Adam Clayton Powell, Jr., New York
Charles C. Diggs, Michigan
Robert N.C. Nix, Pennsylvania
Augustus Hawkins, California

89th Congress, 1965-67

William L. Dawson, Illinois

* Served in Senate, all others House of Representatives

Adam Clayton Powell, Jr., New York
Charles C. Diggs, Michigan
Robert N.C. Nix, Pennsylvania
Augustus Hawkins, California
John Conyers, Jr., Michigan

90th Congress, 1967-69

William L. Dawson, Illinois
Adam Clayton Powell, Jr., New York
Charles C. Diggs, Michigan
Robert N.C. Nix, Pennsylvania
Augustus Hawkins, California
John Conyers, Jr., Michigan
Edward Brooke, Massachusetts*

91st Congress, 1970-72

George W. Collins, Illinois
John Conyers, Jr., Michigan
Ronald V. Dellums, California
Charles C. Diggs, Michigan
Augustus Hawkins, California
Ralph Metcalf, Illinois
Parren J. Mitchell
Robert N.C. Nix, Pennsylvania
Charles B. Rangle, New York
Edward Brooke, Massachusetts*

* Served in Senate, all others House of Representatives

STATISTICAL ABSTRACT OF THE

AFRO-AMERICAN IN THE UNITED STATES

Adapted from, Statistical Abstract
of the United States 1970

U.S. Department of Commerce,
Bureau of the Census

AFRO-AMERICAN STATISTICS

No. 1. Population, by Residence and Race: 1950 to 1969
[In thousands, except percent. As of April. Minus sign (−) denotes decrease]

RESIDENCE AND RACE	POPULATION				AVERAGE ANNUAL PERCENT CHANGE	
	1950 [1]	1960 [1]	1969 Total	1969 Percent	1950–1960	1960–1969
Total	150,527	178,458	200,279	100.0	1.7	1.3
Standard metropolitan statistical areas [2]	89,162	112,901	129,182	64.5	2.4	1.5
Central cities	52,190	57,790	58,553	29.2	1.0	0.1
Outside central cities	36,972	55,111	70,629	35.3	4.0	2.7
Nonmetropolitan areas	61,365	65,557	71,097	35.5	0.7	0.9
Nonfarm	(NA)	165,099	189,970	94.9	(NA)	1.6
Farm	(NA)	13,359	10,309	5.1	(NA)	−2.9
White	134,429	158,051	175,714	100.0	1.6	1.2
Standard metropolitan statistical areas [2]	80,228	99,739	111,998	63.7	2.2	1.3
Central cities	45,322	47,463	45,335	25.8	0.5	−0.5
Outside central cities	34,906	52,276	66,663	37.9	4.0	2.7
Nonmetropolitan areas	54,201	58,312	63,717	36.3	0.7	1.0
Nonfarm	(NA)	146,282	166,406	94.7	(NA)	1.4
Farm	(NA)	11,769	9,307	5.3	(NA)	−2.6
Negro and other	16,098	20,407	24,566	100.0	2.4	2.1
Standard metropolitan statistical areas [2]	8,934	13,161	17,185	70.0	3.9	2.9
Central cities	6,868	10,327	13,219	53.8	4.1	2.7
Outside central cities	2,066	2,834	3,967	16.2	3.2	3.7
Nonmetropolitan areas	7,164	7,246	7,380	30.0	0.1	0.2
Nonfarm	(NA)	18,817	23,564	95.9	(NA)	2.5
Farm	(NA)	1,590	1,002	4.1	(NA)	−5.1
Negro	14,972	18,793	22,419	100.0	2.3	2.0
Standard metropolitan statistical areas [2]	8,325	12,168	15,670	69.9	3.8	2.8
Central cities	6,440	9,687	12,370	55.2	4.1	2.7
Outside central cities	1,885	2,481	3,300	14.7	2.7	3.1
Nonmetropolitan areas	6,647	6,625	6,749	30.1	(Z)	0.2
Nonfarm	(NA)	17,311	21,506	95.9	(NA)	2.4
Farm	(NA)	1,482	913	4.1	(NA)	−5.4

NA Not available. Z Less than 0.05 percent. [1] For comparability with data from the Current Population Survey, figures have been adjusted to exclude members of the Armed Forces living in barracks and similar types of quarters.
[2] Covers 212 areas as defined in 1960;

Source: Dept. of Commerce, Bureau of the Census; *Current Population Reports*, Series P-20, Nos. 157, 163, and 197.

No. 2 POPULATION, URBAN AND RURAL, BY RACE: 1950 AND 1960

[**In thousands, except percent.** An urbanized area comprises at least 1 city of 50,000 inhabitants (central city) plus contiguous, closely settled areas (urban fringe)]

YEAR AND AREA	Total	White	Negro and other	PERCENT DISTRIBUTION		
				Total	White	Negro and other
1950	151,326	135,150	16,176	100.0	100.0	100.0
Urban	96,847	86,864	9,983	64.0	64.3	61.7
Urbanized areas	69,249	61,925	7,324	45.8	45.8	45.3
Central cities	48,377	42,042	6,335	32.0	31.1	39.2
Urban fringe	20,872	19,883	989	13.8	14.7	6.1
Other urban	27,598	24,939	2,659	18.2	18.5	16.4
Rural	54,479	48,286	6,193	36.0	35.7	38.3
1960	179,323	158,832	20,491	100.0	100.0	100.0
Urban	125,269	110,428	14,840	69.9	69.5	72.4
Urbanized areas	95,848	83,770	12,079	53.5	52.7	58.9
Central cities	57,975	47,627	10,348	32.3	30.0	50.5
Urban fringe	37,873	36,143	1,731	21.1	22.8	8.4
Other urban	29,420	26,658	2,762	16.4	16.8	13.5
Rural	54,054	48,403	5,651	30.1	30.5	27.6

Source: Dept. of Commerce, Bureau of the Census; *U.S. Census of Population: 1960*, Vol. I.

AFRO-AMERICAN STATISTICS

No. 3   Negro Population, by Region and Residence: 1940 to 1969

[Prior to 1960, excludes Alaska and Hawaii.]

REGION	1940	1950	1960	1969	RESIDENCE	1950	1960	1969
Percent distribution	100	100	100	100	Population ____millions_	15.0	18.8	22.4
North	22	28	34	41	Metropolitan areas	8.3	12.2	15.8
Northeast	11	13	16	19	Central cities	6.4	9.7	12.5
North Central	11	15	18	21	Urban fringe	1.9	2.5	3.3
South	77	68	60	52	Smaller cities, towns, etc	6.6	6.6	6.6
West	1	4	6	7	Percent distribution	100	100	100
Percent of all classes	10	10	11	11	Metropolitan areas	56	65	71
North	4	5	7	9	Central cities	43	52	56
Northeast	4	5	7	9	Urban fringe	13	13	15
North Central	4	5	7	8	Smaller cities, towns, etc	44	35	29
South	24	22	21	19				
West	1	3	4	5				

Source: Dept. of Commerce, Bureau of the Census, and Dept. of Labor, Bureau of Labor Statistics; *The Social and Economic Status of Negroes in the United States, 1969, Current Population Reports*, Series P-23, No. 29, and BLS Report No. 375.

No. 4   Population, by Sex, Race, Residence, and Median Age: 1790 to 1969

[In thousands, except as indicated. Total resident population excluding Armed Forces abroad.]

YEAR	SEX Male	SEX Female	RACE White	RACE Negro Number	RACE Negro Percent	Other	RESIDENCE[1] Urban	RESIDENCE[1] Rural	MEDIAN AGE (years) All classes	MEDIAN AGE (years) White
CONTERMINOUS U.S.[2]										
1790	(NA)	(NA)	3,172	757	19.3	(NA)	202	3,728	(NA)	(NA)
1800	(NA)	(NA)	4,306	1,002	18.9	(NA)	322	4,986	(NA)	16.0
1810	(NA)	(NA)	5,862	1,378	19.0	(NA)	525	6,714	(NA)	16.0
1820	4,897	4,742	7,867	1,772	18.4	(NA)	693	8,945	16.7	16.5
1830	6,532	6,334	10,537	2,329	18.1	(NA)	1,127	11,739	17.2	17.2
1840	8,689	8,381	14,196	2,874	16.8	(NA)	1,845	15,224	17.8	17.9
1850	11,838	11,354	19,553	3,639	15.7	(NA)	3,544	19,648	18.9	19.2
1860	16,085	15,358	26,923	4,442	14.1	79	6,217	25,227	19.4	19.7
1870	19,494	19,065	33,589	4,880	12.7	89	9,902	28,656	20.2	20.4
1880	25,519	24,637	43,403	6,581	13.1	172	14,130	36,026	20.9	21.4
1890	32,237	30,711	55,101	7,489	11.9	358	22,106	40,841	22.0	22.5
1900	38,816	37,178	66,809	8,834	11.6	351	30,160	45,835	22.9	23.4
1910	47,332	44,640	81,732	9,828	10.7	413	41,999	49,973	24.1	24.5
1920	53,900	51,810	94,821	10,463	9.9	427	54,158	51,553	25.3	25.6
1930	62,137	60,638	110,287	11,891	9.7	597	68,955	53,820	26.4	26.9
1940	66,062	65,608	118,215	12,866	9.8	589	74,424	57,246	29.0	29.5
1950	74,833	75,864	134,942	15,042	10.0	713	96,468	54,230	30.2	30.8
1960	87,865	90,600	158,455	18,860	10.6	1,149	124,699	53,765	29.6	30.3
UNITED STATES										
1950	75,187	76,139	135,150	15,045	9.9	1,131	96,847	54,479	30.2	30.7
1960	88,331	90,992	158,832	18,872	10.5	1,620	125,269	54,054	29.5	30.3
1965[3]	95,110	98,704	170,737	21,147	10.9	1,931	(NA)	(NA)	28.0	29.0
1966[3]	95,969	99,967	172,416	21,519	11.0	2,001	(NA)	(NA)	27.9	28.8
1967[3]	96,688	101,171	173,899	21,869	11.1	2,090	(NA)	(NA)	27.8	28.8
1968[3]	97,542	102,304	175,475	22,210	11.1	2,161	(NA)	(NA)	27.8	28.8
1969[3]	98,482	103,439	177,082	22,596	11.2	2,243	(NA)	(NA)	27.8	28.8

NA Not available.   [1] Beginning 1950, current definition.
[2] Excludes Alaska and Hawaii.   [3] Estimates as of July 1.

Source: Dept. of Commerce, Bureau of the Census; Fifteenth Census Reports, *Population*, Vol. II; Sixteenth Census Reports, *Population*, Vol. II, Part 1, and Vol. IV, Part 1; *U.S. Census of Population: 1950*, Vol. II, Part 1; *U.S. Census of Population: 1960*, Vol. I, and *Current Population Reports*, Series P-25, Nos. 367, 385, and 441.

No. 5 SEX RATIO OF THE POPULATION, BY AGE GROUPS, 1910 TO 1969, AND BY RACE, 1969

[Ratio represents number of males per 100 females. Total resident population]

AGE	1910	1920	1930	1940	1950	1960	1969 [1] Total	White	Negro	Other
All ages	[2] 106.2	[2] 104.1	[2] 102.6	100.8	98.7	97.1	95.2	95.5	92.2	100.3
Under 15 years	102.2	102.1	102.6	103.0	103.7	103.4	103.8	104.4	100.6	103.4
15–24 years	101.2	96.9	98.2	98.7	97.8	98.3	97.6	98.0	95.1	92.7
25–44 years	110.5	105.3	101.0	98.7	96.5	95.7	95.8	97.1	86.4	84.7
45–64 years	114.7	115.4	109.2	105.3	100.2	95.7	91.8	92.3	85.1	121.6
65 years and over	101.2	101.5	100.6	95.7	89.7	82.8	74.2	73.7	77.5	129.9

[1] Estimates as of July 1;
[2] Includes figures for "age not reported."

Source: Dept. of Commerce, Bureau of the Census; based on *U.S. Census of Population: 1950*, and *1960*, Vol. I, and *Current Population Reports*, Series P-25, No. 441.

No. 6 POPULATION, BY AGE, 1930 TO 1960, AND BY RACE, 1950 AND 1960

[In thousands, except as indicated. For definition of median, see preface. See also *Historical Statistics, Colonial Times to 1957*, series A 71–94]

AGE (in years)	1930	1940	1950 Total	1950 White	1950 Other races Total	1950 Other races Negro[1]	1960 Total	1960 White	1960 Other races Total	1960 Other races Negro[1]
Total	[2] 123,203	132,165	151,326	135,150	16,176	15,045	179,323	158,832	20,491	18,849
Under 5	11,499	10,589	16,243	14,207	2,036	1,884	20,321	17,359	2,962	2,722
5–14	24,709	22,535	24,429	21,315	3,115	2,888	35,465	30,727	4,739	4,364
15–24	22,507	24,032	22,220	19,552	2,668	2,462	24,020	21,079	2,941	2,709
25–34	19,026	21,428	23,878	21,330	2,549	2,366	22,818	20,145	2,674	2,406
35–44	17,248	18,393	21,535	19,281	2,253	2,116	24,081	21,564	2,517	2,308
45–54	13,055	15,553	17,398	15,724	1,674	1,568	20,485	18,479	2,006	1,865
55–64	8,418	10,598	13,327	12,359	967	902	15,572	14,177	1,396	1,308
65–74	4,729	6,389	8,432	7,773	660	621	10,997	10,130	867	811
75 and over	1,916	2,647	3,862	3,609	253	238	5,563	5,174	389	356
Median age	26.4	29.0	30.2	30.7	26.0	26.2	29.5	30.3	23.5	23.5

[1] Based on sample; 1950 excludes Alaska and Hawaii. [2] Includes persons for whom age not reported.

Source: Dept. of Commerce, Bureau of the Census; *U.S. Census of Population: 1950*, Vol. IV, Part 3; *1960*, Vol. I, and PC(2)-1C.

AFRO-AMERICAN STATISTICS

No. 7 POPULATION, BY RACE—STATES: 1940 TO 1960

STATE	1940 White	1940 Negro	1940 Other races	1950 White	1950 Negro	1950 Other races	1960 White	1960 Negro Number	1960 Negro Percent of all classes	1960 Other races
U.S.	118,357,831	12,865,914	941,384	135,149,629	15,044,937	1,131,232	158,831,732	18,871,831	10.5	1,619,612
N.E.	8,329,146	101,509	6,635	9,161,156	142,941	10,356	10,242,389	243,363	2.3	23,615
Maine	844,543	1,304	1,379	910,846	1,221	1,707	963,291	3,318	0.3	2,656
N.H.	490,989	414	121	532,275	731	236	604,334	1,903	0.3	684
Vt.	358,806	384	41	377,188	443	116	389,092	519	0.1	270
Mass.	4,257,596	55,391	3,734	4,611,503	73,171	5,840	5,023,144	111,842	2.2	13,592
R.I.	701,805	11,024	517	777,015	13,903	978	838,712	18,332	2.1	2,444
Conn.	1,675,407	32,992	843	1,952,329	53,472	1,479	2,423,816	107,449	4.2	3,969
M.A.	26,237,622	1,268,366	33,499	28,237,528	1,875,241	50,764	31,280,078	2,785,186	8.2	103,238
N.Y.	12,879,546	571,221	28,375	13,872,095	918,191	39,906	15,287,071	1,417,511	8.4	77,722
N.J.	3,931,087	226,973	2,105	4,511,585	318,565	5,179	5,539,003	514,875	8.5	12,904
Pa.	9,426,989	470,172	3,019	9,853,848	638,485	5,679	10,454,004	852,750	7.5	12,612
E.N.C.	25,528,451	1,069,326	28,565	28,543,307	1,803,698	52,363	33,253,272	2,884,969	8.0	86,783
Ohio	6,566,531	339,461	1,620	7,428,222	513,072	5,333	8,909,698	786,097	8.1	10,602
Ind.	3,305,323	121,916	557	3,758,512	174,168	1,544	4,388,554	269,275	5.8	4,669
Ill.	7,504,202	387,446	5,593	8,046,058	645,980	20,138	9,010,252	1,037,470	10.3	33,436
Mich.	5,039,643	208,345	8,118	5,917,825	442,296	11,645	7,085,865	717,581	9.2	19,748
Wis.	3,112,752	12,158	12,677	3,392,690	28,182	13,703	3,858,903	74,546	1.9	18,328
W.N.C.	13,111,519	350,992	54,479	13,576,077	424,178	61,139	14,749,345	561,068	3.6	83,702
Minn.	2,768,982	9,928	13,390	2,953,697	14,022	14,764	3,371,603	22,263	0.7	19,998
Iowa	2,520,691	16,694	883	2,599,546	19,692	1,835	2,728,709	25,354	0.9	3,474
Mo.	3,539,187	244,386	1,091	3,655,593	297,088	1,972	3,922,967	390,853	9.0	5,993
N. Dak.	631,464	201	10,270	608,448	257	10,931	619,538	777	0.1	12,131
S. Dak.	619,075	474	23,412	628,504	727	23,509	653,098	1,114	0.2	26,302
Nebr.	1,297,624	14,171	4,039	1,301,328	19,234	4,948	1,374,764	29,262	2.1	7,304
Kans.	1,734,496	65,138	1,394	1,828,961	73,158	3,180	2,078,666	91,445	4.2	8,500
S.A.	13,095,227	4,698,863	29,061	16,041,709	5,094,744	45,882	20,047,496	5,844,565	22.5	79,671
Del.	230,528	35,876	101	273,878	43,598	609	384,327	60,688	13.6	1,277
Md.	1,518,481	301,931	832	1,954,975	385,972	2,054	2,573,919	518,410	16.7	8,360
D.C.	474,326	187,266	1,499	517,865	280,803	3,510	345,263	411,737	53.9	6,956
Va.	2,015,583	661,449	741	2,581,555	734,211	2,914	3,142,443	816,258	20.6	8,248
W. Va.	1,784,102	117,754	118	1,890,282	114,867	403	1,770,133	89,378	4.8	910
N.C.	2,567,635	981,298	22,690	2,983,121	1,047,353	31,455	3,399,285	1,116,021	24.5	40,849
S.C.	1,084,308	814,164	1,332	1,293,405	822,077	1,545	1,551,022	829,291	34.8	2,281
Ga.	2,038,278	1,084,927	518	2,380,577	1,062,762	1,239	2,817,223	1,122,596	28.5	3,297
Fla.	1,381,986	514,198	1,230	2,166,051	603,101	2,153	4,063,881	880,186	17.8	7,493
E.S.C.	7,993,755	2,780,635	3,835	8,770,570	2,698,635	7,976	9,338,991	2,698,839	22.4	12,296
Ky.	2,631,425	214,031	171	2,742,090	201,921	795	2,820,083	215,949	7.1	2,124
Tenn.	2,406,906	508,736	199	2,760,257	530,603	858	2,977,753	586,876	16.5	2,460
Ala.	1,849,097	983,290	574	2,079,591	979,617	2,535	2,283,609	980,271	30.0	2,860
Miss.	1,106,327	1,074,578	2,891	1,188,632	986,494	3,788	1,257,546	915,743	42.0	4,852
W.S.C.	10,569,596	2,425,121	69,808	12,037,250	2,432,028	68,294	14,090,149	2,768,203	16.3	92,903
Ark.	1,466,084	482,578	725	1,481,507	426,639	1,365	1,395,703	388,787	21.8	1,782
La.	1,511,739	849,303	2,838	1,796,683	882,428	4,405	2,211,715	1,039,207	31.9	6,100
Okla.	2,104,228	168,849	63,357	2,032,526	145,503	55,322	2,107,900	153,084	6.6	67,300
Tex.	5,487,545	924,391	2,888	6,726,534	977,458	7,202	8,374,831	1,187,125	12.4	17,721
Mt.	3,978,913	36,411	134,679	4,845,634	66,429	162,935	6,514,294	123,242	1.8	217,524
Mont.	540,468	1,120	17,868	572,038	1,232	17,754	650,738	1,467	0.2	22,562
Idaho	519,292	595	4,986	581,395	1,050	6,192	657,383	1,502	0.2	8,306
Wyo.	246,597	956	3,189	284,009	2,557	3,963	322,922	2,183	0.7	4,961
Colo.	1,106,502	12,176	4,618	1,296,653	20,177	8,259	1,700,700	39,992	2.3	13,255
N. Mex.	492,312	4,672	34,834	630,211	8,408	42,568	875,763	17,063	1.8	58,197
Ariz.	426,792	14,993	57,476	654,511	25,974	69,102	1,169,517	43,403	3.3	89,241
Utah	542,920	1,235	6,155	676,909	2,729	9,224	873,828	4,148	0.5	12,651
Nev.	104,030	664	5,553	149,908	4,302	5,873	263,443	13,484	4.7	8,351
Pac.	9,513,602	134,691	580,823	13,936,398	507,043	671,523	19,315,718	962,446	4.5	919,880
Wash.	1,698,147	7,424	30,620	2,316,496	30,691	31,776	2,751,675	48,738	1.7	52,801
Oreg.	1,075,731	2,565	11,388	1,497,128	11,529	12,684	1,732,037	18,133	1.0	18,517
Calif.	6,596,763	124,306	186,318	9,915,173	462,172	208,878	14,455,230	883,861	5.6	378,113
Alaska	39,170	141	33,213	92,808	(1)	35,835	174,546	6,771	3.0	44,850
Hawaii	103,791	255	319,284	114,793	2,651	382,350	202,230	4,943	0.8	425,599

[1] Not identified separately.

Source: Dept. of Commerce, Bureau of the Census; Sixteenth Census Reports, *Population*, Vol. II, *U.S. Census of Population: 1950*, Vol. II, Part 1, and *U.S. Census of Population: 1960*, Vol. I.

No. 8 SELECTED CHARACTERISTICS OF FAMILIES, BY RACE: 1967 TO 1969

As of March.

CHARACTERISTICS	1967 White	1967 Negro	1968 White	1968 Negro	1969 White	1969 Negro
All families 1,000	44,110	4,560	44,814	4,589	45,437	4,646
Female head 1,000	4,032	1,138	4,008	1,272	4,053	1,327
Percent of all families	9.1	25.0	8.9	27.7	8.9	28.6
Own children under age 18 per family	1.30	1.76	1.29	1.78	1.27	1.80
Female head	0.98	1.93	1.01	1.98	1.03	1.95
Percent of children of family heads living with both parents	92.4	71.0	92.2	67.3	91.9	67.2
Percent distribution, by marital status of female head:						
Separated	12.0	33.3	12.0	34.6	12.0	36.9
Other married, husband absent	7.4	7.3	7.0	5.1	7.7	5.6
Widowed	49.6	34.7	50.1	33.4	47.5	31.2
Divorced	21.9	13.3	21.9	13.1	22.8	12.8
Single	9.1	11.6	8.9	13.8	9.8	13.6

Source: Dept. of Commerce, Bureau of the Census; *Current Population Reports*, Series P-20.

No. 9 EXPECTATION OF LIFE AT BIRTH: 1920 TO 1967

[In years. Prior to 1960, excludes Alaska and Hawaii. Data prior to 1933 for death-registration States only; See also *Historical Statistics, Colonial Times to 1957*, series B 92-100]

YEAR	TOTAL Total	TOTAL Male	TOTAL Female	WHITE Total	WHITE Male	WHITE Female	NEGRO AND OTHER Total	NEGRO AND OTHER Male	NEGRO AND OTHER Female
1920	54.1	53.6	54.6	54.9	54.4	55.6	45.3	45.5	45.2
1930	59.7	58.1	61.6	61.4	59.7	63.5	48.1	47.3	49.2
1940	62.9	60.8	65.2	64.2	62.1	66.6	53.1	51.5	54.9
1950	68.2	65.6	71.1	69.1	66.5	72.2	60.8	59.1	62.9
1955	69.5	66.6	72.7	70.2	67.3	73.6	63.2	61.2	65.9
1960	69.7	66.6	73.1	70.6	67.4	74.1	63.6	61.1	66.3
1965	70.2	66.8	73.7	71.0	67.6	74.7	64.1	61.1	67.4
1966	70.1	66.7	73.8	71.0	67.6	74.7	64.0	60.7	67.4
1967	70.5	67.0	74.2	71.3	67.8	75.1	64.6	61.1	68.2

Source: Dept. of Health, Education, and Welfare, Public Health Service; annual report, *Vital Statistics of the United States*.

No. 10. School Enrollment, by Race, Level of School, and Age: 1960 and 1969

In thousands, except percent. As of October.

AGE	WHITE				NEGRO AND OTHER			
	Total enrolled	Elementary [1]	High school [1]	College [1]	Total enrolled	Elementary [1]	High school [1]	College [1]
1960								
Total, 5–34 years	40,348	27,884	9,122	3,342	5,910	4,556	1,127	227
5–13 years	27,723	27,149	574	–	4,336	4,285	51	–
14–17 years	9,028	731	8,084	214	1,213	268	937	8
18–24 years	2,854	4	431	2,420	312	2	132	178
25–34 years	743	1	33	709	49	1	7	41
1969								
Total, 5–34 years	50,531	31,117	12,588	6,827	8,187	5,614	1,966	607
5–13 years	30,627	30,237	394	–	5,372	5,318	56	–
14–17 years	12,489	860	11,407	222	1,962	294	1,648	20
18–24 years	6,006	5	654	5,347	724	1	230	493
25–34 years	1,408	17	131	1,259	128	4	30	95
Percent change, 1960–1969	25.2	11.6	38.0	104.3	38.5	23.2	74.2	167.4

– Represents zero. [1] Elementary includes kindergarten and nursery schools; high school, grades 9–12; college includes professional schools.

Source of tables 153 and 154: Dept. of Commerce, Bureau of the Census; *Current Population Reports*, Series P-20, and unpublished data.

No. 11. Years of School Completed, by Race: 1947 to 1969

[Persons 25 years old and over as of March of year indicated, except as noted. Based on Current Population Survey; includes inmates of institutions and members of the Armed Forces living off post or with their families on post, but excludes all other members of the Armed Forces; see text, p. 1]

AGE AND YEAR	ALL RACES				NEGRO AND OTHER (except white)			
	Elementary school, less than 5 years [1]	High school, 4 years or more	College, 4 years or more	Median school years completed [2]	Elementary school, less than 5 years [1]	High school, 4 years or more	College, 4 years or more	Median school years completed [2]
25 YEARS AND OVER								
1947 [3]	10.6	33.1	5.4	9.0	32.2	13.6	2.5	6.9
1957	9.1	41.6	7.6	10.6	27.7	18.4	2.9	7.7
1960	8.3	41.1	7.7	10.5	23.5	21.7	3.5	8.2
1965	6.8	49.0	9.4	11.8	18.4	28.6	5.5	9.0
1968	5.9	52.6	10.5	12.1	17.3	32.5	5.5	9.5
1969	5.6	54.0	10.7	12.1	15.2	34.5	6.0	9.8
25–29 YEARS								
1947 [3]	4.3	51.4	5.6	12.0	19.2	22.3	2.8	8.4
1957	2.7	60.2	10.4	12.3	8.7	31.6	4.1	9.9
1960	2.8	60.7	11.1	12.3	7.2	38.6	5.4	10.8
1965	2.0	70.3	12.4	12.4	4.8	52.2	8.3	12.1
1968	1.1	73.2	14.7	12.5	2.8	57.6	7.9	12.2
1969	1.3	74.7	16.0	12.6	2.5	57.5	9.1	12.2

[1] Includes persons reporting no school years completed.
[2] For definition of median, see preface. [3] As of April.

Source: Dept. of Commerce, Bureau of the Census; *Current Population Reports*, Series P-20, No. 194.

BLACKS IN AMERICA

No. 12 Employment Status of the Noninstitutional Population, by Sex and Race: 1950 to 1970

[In thousands of persons 16 years old and over, except as noted. Prior to 1960, excludes Alaska and Hawaii. Annual figures are averages of monthly figures. See *Historical Statistics, Colonial Times to 1957*, series D 1–14 and D 20, for similar but not exactly comparable data]

YEAR OR MONTH, SEX, AND RACE	Total noninstitutional population	Total, including Armed Forces	Civilian labor force Total	Percent of population	Employed Total	Employed Agricultural	Employed Non-agricultural	Unemployed Number	Unemployed Percent	Not in labor force Total [1]	Keeping house [2]	In school [2]
TOTAL												
1950	106,645	63,858	62,208	58.3	58,920	7,160	51,760	3,288	5.3	42,787	33,058	6,197
1955	112,732	68,072	65,023	57.7	62,171	6,449	55,724	2,852	4.4	44,660	33,722	6,569
1960	119,759	72,142	69,628	58.1	65,778	5,458	60,318	3,852	5.5	47,617	34,543	8,162
1963	125,154	74,571	71,833	57.4	67,762	4,687	63,076	4,070	5.7	50,583	35,322	10,099
1964	127,224	75,830	73,091	57.5	69,305	4,523	64,782	3,786	5.2	51,394	35,454	10,510
1965	129,236	77,178	74,455	57.6	71,088	4,361	66,726	3,366	4.5	52,058	35,556	11,094
1966	131,180	78,893	75,770	57.8	72,895	3,979	68,915	2,875	3.8	52,288	35,316	11,148
1967	133,320	80,793	77,347	58.0	74,372	3,844	70,528	2,975	3.8	52,527	34,993	6,657
1968	135,562	82,272	78,737	58.1	75,920	3,817	72,103	2,817	3.6	53,291	35,204	6,900
1969	137,841	84,239	80,733	58.6	77,902	3,606	74,296	2,831	3.5	53,602	34,888	7,013
1970, Apr	139,687	85,231	81,960	58.7	78,408	3,531	74,877	3,552	4.3	54,456	34,671	8,933
MALE												
1950	52,352	45,446	43,819	83.7	41,580	6,001	35,578	2,239	5.1	6,906	81	3,244
1955	55,122	47,488	44,475	80.7	42,621	5,265	37,357	1,854	4.2	7,634	76	3,313
1960	58,144	48,870	46,388	79.8	43,904	4,472	39,431	2,486	5.4	9,274	87	4,097
1963	60,627	49,835	47,129	77.7	44,657	3,809	40,849	2,472	5.2	10,792	136	5,077
1964	61,556	50,387	47,679	77.5	45,474	3,691	41,782	2,205	4.6	11,169	139	5,219
1965	62,473	50,946	48,255	77.2	46,340	3,547	42,792	1,914	4.0	11,527	143	5,517
1966	63,351	51,560	48,471	76.5	46,919	3,243	43,675	1,551	3.2	11,792	120	5,597
1967	64,316	52,398	48,987	76.2	47,479	3,164	44,315	1,508	3.1	11,919	142	3,326
1968	65,345	53,030	49,533	75.8	48,114	3,157	44,957	1,419	2.9	12,315	180	3,492
1969	66,365	53,688	50,221	75.7	48,818	2,963	45,854	1,403	2.8	12,677	199	3,570
1970, Apr	67,183	53,899	50,667	75.4	48,686	2,979	45,708	1,981	3.9	13,284	225	4,493
Negro and other: [3]												
1955	[4] 5,326	(NA)	4,358	81.8	4,001	710	3,290	357	8.2	968	(NA)	(NA)
1960	[4] 5,952	(NA)	4,728	79.4	4,220	657	3,563	508	10.7	1,223	(NA)	(NA)
1963	[4] 6,335	(NA)	4,802	75.8	4,293	527	3,766	509	10.6	1,533	(NA)	(NA)
1964	[4] 6,439	(NA)	4,871	75.6	4,429	497	3,932	443	9.1	1,568	18	639
1965	[4] 6,576	(NA)	4,945	75.2	4,568	493	4,075	377	7.6	1,631	23	680
1966	[4] 6,686	(NA)	4,983	74.5	4,655	392	4,264	328	6.6	1,703	18	719
1967	6,606	5,253	4,945	74.9	4,646	361	4,285	299	6.0	1,353	19	429
1968	6,755	5,322	4,979	73.7	4,702	353	4,350	277	5.6	1,434	25	453
1969	6,918	5,404	5,036	72.8	4,770	309	4,461	266	5.3	1,513	34	480
1970, Apr	7,054	5,414	5,092	72.2	4,750	290	4,459	342	6.7	1,639	45	633
FEMALE												
1950	54,293	18,412	18,389	33.9	17,340	1,159	16,182	1,049	5.7	35,881	32,977	2,954
1955	57,610	20,584	20,548	35.7	19,550	1,184	18,367	998	4.9	37,026	33,646	3,256
1960	61,615	23,272	23,240	37.7	21,874	986	20,887	1,366	5.9	38,343	34,456	4,065
1963	64,527	24,736	24,704	38.3	23,105	878	22,227	1,598	6.5	39,791	35,185	5,021
1964	65,668	25,443	25,412	38.7	23,831	832	23,000	1,581	6.2	40,225	35,316	5,291
1965	66,763	26,232	26,200	39.2	24,748	814	23,934	1,452	5.5	40,531	35,413	5,577
1966	67,829	27,333	27,299	40.2	25,976	736	25,240	1,324	4.8	40,496	35,155	5,551
1967	69,003	28,395	28,360	41.1	26,893	680	26,212	1,468	5.2	40,608	34,851	3,331
1968	70,217	29,242	29,204	41.6	27,808	660	27,147	1,397	4.8	40,976	35,023	3,408
1969	71,476	30,551	30,512	42.7	29,084	643	28,441	1,428	4.7	40,924	34,688	3,443
1970, Apr	72,504	31,332	31,293	43.2	29,722	553	29,169	1,571	5.0	41,172	34,446	4,439
Negro and other: [3]												
1955	[4] 6,069	(NA)	2,697	44.4	2,495	310	2,185	202	7.5	3,372	(NA)	(NA)
1960	[4] 6,726	(NA)	3,116	46.3	2,821	277	2,544	295	9.5	3,610	(NA)	(NA)
1963	[4] 7,271	(NA)	3,318	45.6	2,941	221	2,720	376	11.3	3,954	(NA)	(NA)
1964	[4] 7,437	(NA)	3,421	46.0	3,052	190	2,861	369	10.8	4,016	2,970	700
1965	[4] 7,609	(NA)	3,503	46.0	3,179	181	2,998	324	9.3	4,106	3,017	765
1966	[4] 7,784	(NA)	3,634	46.7	3,313	136	3,177	321	8.8	4,150	3,001	790
1967	7,479	3,706	3,704	49.5	3,366	104	3,262	338	9.1	3,773	2,967	456
1968	7,670	3,784	3,780	49.3	3,467	90	3,377	313	8.3	3,886	3,041	467
1969	7,877	3,922	3,918	49.7	3,614	78	3,536	304	7.8	3,955	3,044	511
1970, Apr	8,055	3,999	3,996	49.6	3,646	40	3,606	349	8.7	4,056	3,013	675

NA Not available. [1] Includes "other", not shown separately. [2] 1950–1966, persons 14 years old and over. [3] Excludes white. [4] Civilian noninstitutional population.

Source: Dept. of Labor, Bureau of Labor Statistics; monthly report, *Employment and Earnings*.

AFRO-AMERICAN STATISTICS 141

No. **13** UNEMPLOYED, PART-TIME EMPLOYED, AND UNEMPLOYMENT INSURANCE—SUMMARY: 1955 TO 1970

[Persons 16 years old and over. Prior to 1960, excludes Alaska and Hawaii. See *Historical Statistics, Colonial Times to 1957*, series D 46 and 47, for total unemployed and rate]

SUBJECT	1955	1960	1965	1966	1967	1968	1969	1970, April
Total, unemployed _____ 1,000__	2,852	3,852	3,366	2,875	2,975	2,817	2,831	3,552
Labor force time lost [1] _____ percent__	[2] 4.8	6.7	5.0	4.2	4.2	4.0	3.9	5.1
Male _____ 1,000__	1,854	2,486	1,914	1,551	1,508	1,419	1,403	1,981
Female _____ 1,000__	998	1,366	1,452	1,324	1,468	1,397	1,428	1,517
Race:								
White _____ 1,000__	2,248	3,063	2,691	2,253	2,338	2,226	2,261	2,861
Negro and other _____ 1,000__	601	787	676	621	638	590	570	619
Age and sex:								
16-19 years _____ 1,000__	450	711	874	836	838	839	853	883
Percent of total unemployed	15.8	18.5	26.0	29.1	28.2	29.8	30.1	24.9
White _____ 1,000__	(NA)	(NA)	(NA)	651	635	644	660	703
Negro and other _____ 1,000__	(NA)	(NA)	(NA)	185	204	195	193	180
Male _____ 1,000__	274	425	479	432	448	427	441	483
Female _____ 1,000__	176	286	395	404	391	412	412	400
20-24 years _____ 1,000__	396	583	557	445	512	543	560	705
Percent of total unemployed	13.9	15.1	16.5	15.5	17.2	19.3	19.8	19.8
Male _____ 1,000__	248	369	311	221	235	258	270	389
Female _____ 1,000__	148	214	246	224	277	285	290	316
25-44 years _____ 1,000__	1,098	1,423	1,076	865	902	813	810	1,104
Percent of total unemployed	38.5	36.9	32.0	30.1	30.3	28.9	28.6	31.1
Male _____ 1,000__	681	907	577	457	404	376	360	592
Female _____ 1,000__	417	516	499	408	498	437	450	512
45-64 years _____ 1,000__	791	1,009	758	636	641	534	536	762
Percent of total unemployed	27.7	26.2	22.5	22.1	21.5	19.0	18.9	21.5
Male _____ 1,000__	550	686	474	377	363	297	284	453
Female _____ 1,000__	241	323	284	259	278	236	252	309
65 years and over _____ 1,000__	120	121	102	92	86	88	72	97
Percent of total unemployed	4.2	3.1	3.0	3.2	2.9	2.8	2.5	2.7
Unemployment rate (percent): [3]								
All workers _____	4.4	5.5	4.5	3.8	3.8	3.6	3.5	4.3
White _____	3.9	4.9	4.1	3.3	3.4	3.2	3.1	3.9
Male _____	3.7	4.8	3.6	2.8	2.7	2.6	2.5	3.6
Female _____	4.3	5.3	5.0	4.3	4.6	4.3	4.2	4.5
Negro and other _____	8.7	10.2	8.1	7.3	7.4	6.7	6.4	7.6
Male _____	8.8	10.7	7.4	6.3	6.0	5.6	5.3	6.7
Female _____	8.4	9.4	9.2	8.6	9.1	8.3	7.8	8.7
Ratio, nonwhite to white _____	2.2	2.1	2.0	2.2	2.2	2.1	2.1	1.9
Blue-collar workers _____	(NA)	(NA)	(NA)	(NA)	4.4	4.1	3.9	5.7
White-collar workers _____	(NA)	(NA)	(NA)	(NA)	2.2	2.0	2.1	2.5
Experienced wage and salary workers ___	(NA)	(NA)	(NA)	(NA)	3.6	3.4	3.3	4.2
Married men, wife present _____	(NA)	(NA)	(NA)	(NA)	1.8	1.6	1.5	2.4
White _____	(NA)	(NA)	(NA)	(NA)	1.7	1.5	1.4	2.3
Negro and other _____	(NA)	(NA)	(NA)	(NA)	3.2	2.9	2.5	3.7
Percent without work for—								
4 weeks or less _____	46.8	44.6	48.4	53.4	54.9	56.6	57.5	51.7
5-10 weeks _____	21.0	21.4	21.0	20.8	22.6	21.8	22.1	18.6
11-14 weeks _____	7.6	9.2	8.2	7.2	7.3	7.0	7.1	8.0
15-26 weeks _____	12.9	13.0	12.0	10.3	9.1	9.1	8.5	15.1
Over 26 weeks _____	11.8	11.8	10.4	8.4	5.9	5.5	4.7	6.6
Average duration of unemployment _____ wks__	(NA)	(NA)	(NA)	(NA)	8.8	8.5	7.9	9.5
Part-time employed [4] _____ 1,000__	(NA)	(NA)	(NA)	1,894	2,163	1,970	2,055	2,301
Unemployment insurance: [5]								
Weekly insured unemployment, avg. [6] __ 1,000__	1,254	1,906	1,328	1,061	1,205	1,111	1,101	1,770
Percent of covered employment [6] _____	3.5	4.8	3.0	2.3	2.5	2.2	2.1	3.4
Initial claims (weekly average) [7] _____ 1,000__	226	331	232	203	226	201	200	298
Claimants exhausting benefits [8] _____ 1,000__	1,272	1,603	1,086	781	867	848	812	100
Percent of first payment beneficiaries ___	28.2	23.7	22.6	18.9	19.3	19.6	19.8	18.5
Average actual duration of benefits ____ wks__	12.4	12.7	12.2	11.2	11.4	11.6	11.4	(X)

NA Not available. X Not applicable. [1] Man-hours lost by the unemployed and persons on part-time for economic reasons as a percent of potentially available labor force man-hours. [2] Average of 8 months. [3] Percent of civilian labor force in specified group. [4] Persons who work less than 35 hours during survey week for economic reasons, such as slack work, material shortages or repairs, new job started, job terminated, or only part-time work found. Excludes pers ns with a job but not at work because of vacation, illness, bad weather, or industrial dispute. [5] Source: Dept. of Labor, Manpower Administration, State programs only; excludes programs for Federal employees and for ex-servicemen; includes unemployment compensation for State and local government employees where covered by State law. [6] Workers reporting completion of at least 1 week of unemployment. [7] Notices filed by workers to indicate they are starting periods of unemployment. Excludes transitional claims. [8] Includes temporary extended benefit exhaustions.

Source: Dept. of Labor, Bureau of Labor Statistics; annual report, *Handbook of Labor Statistics* and monthly report, *Employment and Earnings*, except as noted.

No. **14**. Civilian Labor Force and Unemployment, by Race—Regions and 10 Largest States: 1968

Covers persons 16 years old and over. Annual averages based on information collected by Bureau of the Census as part of the Current Population Survey.

RACE, REGION, AND STATE	Civilian labor force [1] (1,000)	Participation rates [2]	Unemployment Number [3] (1,000)	Unemployment Rate [4]	RACE, REGION, AND STATE	Civilian labor force [1] (1,000)	Participation rates [2]	Unemployment Number [3] (1,000)	Unemployment Rate [4]
United States	**78,740**	**59.6**	**2,815**	**3.6**	North Central—Con. E.N.C.—Con.				
White	69,980	59.3	2,225	3.2	Michigan	3,420	59.9	135	3.9
All other	8,760	62.2	590	6.7	White	3,060	59.8	105	3.4
Northeast	19,570	58.9	620	3.2	All other	360	60.1	30	8.2
White	17,980	58.5	530	3.0	West North Central	6,330	60.4	155	2.4
All other	1,580	63.9	90	5.7	White	6,060	60.3	135	2.2
New England	4,950	61.7	145	2.9	All other	270	63.4	20	6.8
White	4,800	61.5	140	2.9	South	23,430	59.4	880	3.7
All other	150	68.4	5	4.5	White	19,080	58.9	590	3.1
Massachusetts	2,230	60.5	65	2.9	All other	4,350	61.6	290	6.6
White	2,150	60.4	60	2.8	South Atlantic	11,770	60.0	420	3.6
All other	80	63.3	(B)	(B)	White	9,320	59.0	275	2.9
Middle Atlantic	14,620	60.5	475	3.2	All other	2,450	64.2	150	6.0
White	13,180	60.4	395	3.0	Florida	2,260	54.9	85	3.8
All other	1,440	61.5	85	5.8	White	1,920	53.4	65	3.3
New York	7,230	57.9	230	3.1	All other	340	65.1	20	6.0
White	6,500	57.6	195	3.0	East South Central	4,780	57.9	200	4.2
All other	740	62.2	30	4.3	White	3,990	58.4	140	3.6
Pennsylvania	4,630	57.1	155	3.4	All other	800	55.4	60	7.5
White	4,240	56.6	125	3.0	West South Central	6,870	59.3	255	3.7
All other	390	62.7	30	7.3	White	5,780	59.0	175	3.0
New Jersey	2,870	59.7	95	3.3	All other	1,100	61.0	80	7.4
White	2,550	58.8	70	2.8	Texas	4,300	61.2	145	3.4
All other	320	67.7	25	7.3	White	3,700	60.6	110	2.9
North Central	22,610	60.5	680	3.0	All other	600	65.4	35	6.0
White	20,920	60.4	545	2.6	West	13,160	59.9	645	4.9
All other	1,680	61.5	135	8.0	White	12,000	59.5	565	4.7
East North Central	16,280	60.5	525	3.2	All other	1,150	63.6	80	6.8
White	14,860	60.4	410	2.8	Mountain	2,920	59.5	125	4.4
All other	1,420	61.1	115	8.2	White	2,800	59.5	120	4.2
Illinois	4,490	61.1	130	2.9	All other	120	59.7	10	7.8
White	4,020	61.4	95	2.3	Pacific	10,240	59.9	520	5.1
All other	460	58.0	35	7.7	White	9,210	59.5	450	4.9
Ohio	4,160	59.0	145	3.4	All other	1,030	64.0	70	6.7
White	3,790	58.7	110	2.9	California	7,570	59.9	390	5.1
All other	370	62.5	35	9.1	White	6,810	59.4	330	4.8
					All other	760	64.5	60	7.9

B Not computed; unemployment estimate less than 5,000.
[1] Figures rounded to nearest 10,000.   [2] Percent of each group in civilian labor force.
[3] Figures rounded to nearest 5,000.   [4] Percent of civilian labor force.

Source: Dept. of Labor, Bureau of Labor Statistics; *Monthly Labor Review*, January 1970.

INDEX

Abbott, Robert S., 20, 25
Abernathy, Rev. Ralph D., 57, 60, 61
Adams, John Quincy, 13
Aldridge, Ira F., 8, 11
Alexander, Clifford, Jr., 60
Allen, Macon B., 14
Allen, Richard, 3, 7, 9
Amistad, 13
Anderson, Rev. Benjamin J., 48
Anderson, Marian, 32, 40, 48
Angola, Antony van and Lucie, 2
Armstrong, Louis, 24, 27
Armstrong, Samuel C., 50
Ashe, Arthur, 48, 58
Ashford, E.L., 39
Attucks, Crispus, 3, 4

Baker, Bertram L., 52
Baker, Gene, 44
Balboa, 1
Baldwin, James, 47
Banneker, Benjamin, 3, 6, 8
Bannister, E.M., 22
Barnett, Gov. Ross R., 46
Barton, Clara, 17
Bates, Mrs. Daisy, 41
Beckwourth, James P., 7, 14
Beecher, Henry Ward, 9
Bell, James Madison, 11
Benezet, Anthony, 2
Bennett, Ebenezer D.C., 20
Bennett, Lerone, Jr., 52
Bethune, Mary McLeod, 21, 29, 31, 40
Bilbo, Senator Theodore C., 32
Blair, Henry, 12

Blanc, Antoine, 6
Bland, James A., 33
"Blind Tom", 15
Blyden, Edward W., 12
Bolin, Matilda J., 32
Boone, John W., 19
Bounchet, Edward A., 22
Braithwaite, William S., 26, 45
Branch, Dr. Mary E., 34
Brawley, Benjamin, 22
Breathitt, Gov. Edward, 51
Brewer, Gov. Albert P., 63
Brewster, Kingman, Jr., 64
Brimmer, Andrew, 53
Brooke, Edwin W., 46, 54, 55, 62
Brooks, L. Clark, 23
Brooks, Walter H., 15
Brooks, Bishop W. Sampson, 31
Brown, Anne, 34
Brown v. Board of Education et. al, 39
Brown, John, 7, 16
Brown, "Rap", 55
Brown, Wesley A., 36
Brown, William Wells, 15, 16, 23
Bruce, Blanche K., 13, 21, 22, 24
Bryan, Andrew, 4, 6
Bunche, Dr. Ralph J., 25, 36, 37, 38, 48, 51, 66
Burleigh, Harry T., 26, 27
Burns, Anthony, 16, 18
Burroughs, Nannie, 25
Bush, Charles V., 39
Butler, General B.F., 17

Cable, George Washington, 23
Calhoun, John C., 10

Campanella, Roy, 59
Carey, Rev. A.J., Jr., 41
Carey, Lott, 5, 10, 11
Carlos, John, 58
Carmichael, Stokely, 53
Carroll, Diahann, 47
Carswell, Judge G. Harrold, 63, 64
Carver, George Washington, 18, 27, 33, 34, 38
Casas, Los Bishop, 1
Chamberlain, Wilt, 47
Chapman, Maria Weston, 8
Chestnutt, Charles W., 16, 24, 29
Chisholm, Shirley, 58
Cinque, 13
Clark, Dr. Felton G., 66
Clark, Kenneth B., 44
Clark, Ramsey, 58
Clay, Cassius M., 8
Clay, Henry, 10
Cleaver, Eldridge, 59
Clement, E.C., 35
Clothide, 17
Coffin, Levi, 7
Cole, Nat "King", 51
Collins, C.W., 30
Collins, George W., 67
Conyers, John H., 21
Conyers, John, Jr., 58
Cook, Marvin, 43
Cook, Will Marion, 20, 35
Cornish, Samuel, 6, 11, 17
Craft, William and Ellen, 15
Creole, 14
Crocket, Sergeant, 19
Cromwell, Oliver, 5
Crummell, Alexander, 10
Cuffee, Paul, 3, 10
Cullen, Countee, 25, 27, 35

Davis, Allison, 65
Davis, Benjamin O., Sr., 33
Davis, Benajmin, Jr., 39, 63
Davis, Ernie, 44
Davis, Sgt. Rodney M., 59

Davis, Tommy, 48
Dawson, William L., 34
De Preist, Oscar, 21, 29, 38
De Soto, 1
Delaney, Martin R., 9
Dellums, Ronald V., 67
Dent, Albert W., 39
Derham, James, 4, 7
Dobbs, Mattiwalda, 45
Dodge, William E., 8
Douglass, Frederick, 10, 12, 13, 14, 15, 22, 23, 24, 27, 35
Drew, Dr. Charles R., 25, 27, 34, 37
Du Bois, W.E.B., 20, 24, 25, 27, 31
Dumas, Alexander, 7
Dunbar, Paul Laurence, 21, 25
Duncan, John, 44
Duncan, Todd, 34
Dunn, Oscar, J., 20
Dunmore, Lord, 4
Dykes, Evan B., 27

Edwards, James, 62
Eisenhower, Pres. Dwight D., 41
Ellington, Edward Kennedy ("Duke"), 24, 42
Elliott, Robert B., 14, 23
Estevanico (Little Stephen), 1
Evans, Rev. E.H., 55
Evans, Dr. Melvin H., 67
Evers, Charles, 60
Evers, Medger, 48, 50

Fauset, Crystal Bird, 52
Flipper, Henry O, 22
Foreman, James, 60, 61
Forten, James, 10, 14, 18
Fortune, Timothy F., 19
Francis, W.T., 29
Franklin, Benjamin, 4
Franklin, John Hope, 40, 45, 48
Frazier, E. Franklin, 45
Fuller, Meta Vaux, 22

INDEX

Garnet, Henry Highland, 9, 14, 19
Garreson, William Lloyd, 11, 22
Garvey, Marcus, 27, 33
Gibson, Althea, 37, 41
Gibson, Kenneth A., 65
Gilpin, Charles, 27, 30
Gloucester, Rev. John, 10
Godwin, Gov. Mills E., Jr., 59
Goldwater, Barry, 48
Goode, Mel, 46
Goodloe, Daniel Reaves, 9
Grandy, Samuel L., 45
Grant, Earl, 65
Greener, Richard T., 21
Griffin, Edward, 5
Grimke, Archibald, 15, 27
Groppi, Rev. Joseph, 54
Guinn v. U.S., 26

Hall, Lt. Charles, 34
Hall, Prince, 3
Hamilton, Mary, 49
Hammon, Jupiter, 3, 4
Hampton, Fred, 62, 63
Handy, W.C., 21, 25
Hansberry, Lorraine, 42, 51
Harper, Frances Allen Watkins, 11
Harrison, Richard B., 19, 29, 30, 31
Hastie, William H., 31, 34, 35, 37
Hatcher, Richard G., 56, 58
Hawkins, August, 46
Hawkins, John, 1
Hayes, Roland, 27
Haynsworth, Clement F., 62
Healy, James A., 11, 24
Healy, Patrick Henry, 19, 21
Henderson, Fletcher, 27
Henry, Robert C., 52
Henson, Josiah, 6, 25
Henson, Matthew A., 19
Higginbotham, A. Leon, 46
Higginson, Thomas W., 11
Hocult, Thomas, 30
Holiday, Billie, 42

Holmes, John Haynes, 50
Hope, John, 20, 31
Houston, Charles E., 24, 37
Houston, W.E., 45
Howard, D.E., 32
Hubert, James H., 65
Hughes, Langston, 43
Hunt, Henry A., 29

Ickins, William, 22
Ingram, Rex, 62

Jack, Hulan, 39
Jackson, General Andrew, 9
Jackson, Luther P., 23
Jackson, Peter, 23
James, Rev. S.H., 52
Jefferson, Thomas, 6
Jenkins, Howard, 46
"Jim Crow", 11, 22
Jogner, Rev. Henry, Jr., 65
Johnson, President Andrew, 19
Johnson, Charles S., 27
Johnson, Edward A., 26
Johnson, Henry, 27
Johnson, Jack, 25
Johnson, James Weldon, 21, 27, 32, 37
Johnson, John, 9
Johnson, Leroy, 46
Johnson, President Lyndon B., 51, 52, 54, 57
Johnson, Mordecai Wyatt, 29
Johnson, Mrs. Violette A., 22
Jones, Absalom, 3, 9, 10
Jones, Col. Daniel J., 63
Jones, Hilary H., 59
Jones, James Earl, 58
Jones, Raymond J., 52
Julian, Dr. Percy L., 36
Just, Ernest E., 23, 26

Kennedy, Pres. John F., 44, 48
King, Martin Luther, Jr., 29, 38, 41, 42, 46, 49, 54, 55, 56, 57, 59, 63

Kirk, Gov. Claude R., 63, 64
Knox, Clinton E., 50
Koontz, Mrs. Elizabeth D., 55
Koscuisko, Thaddeus, 7

Lamb, Gerald, 47
Lane, Bishop Isaac, 12, 32
Lane, Lunsford, 7, 13
Laney, Lucey C., 16
Langston, John Mercer, 11, 24
Latimore, George, 14
Lawless, Theodore K.; 39
Lawson, Marjorie, 47
Lee, Howard, 60
Lee, General Robert E., 19
Leftenant, Lt. Nancy C., 36
Leidesdorff, William A., 15
Leile, George, 4
Lewis, Henry, 43, 56
Lewis, John, 53
Lincoln, Abraham, 8, 17, 19
Little, Stephen, 26
Locke, Alaine L., 25
Lomax, Louis E., 66
Lopez, Hector, 59
Louis, Joe (Barrow), 26, 31, 32
L'ouverture, Toussaint, 3, 7
Lovejoy, Elijah P., 13
Lowry, S.R., 11
Lucy, Autherine, 40
Lundy, Benjamin, 6, 13
Lynch, John Roy, 23

Maddox, Gov. Lester, 63, 65
Mansfield, Lord, 4
Marshall, Thurgood, 25, 35, 44, 46, 56
Mason, Louis, Jr., 67
Mason, William T., Jr., 48
Matzeliger, Jan, 22
McClellan, George B., 17
McCoy, Elijah P., 14
McCullough, Geraldine, 51

McKay, Claude, 36
McKethen, Gov. John J., 63
McKissick, Floyd B., 52
Mendez, 1
Meredith, James H., 44, 46, 53, 55
Merrick, John, 24
Metcalfe, Ralph, 67
Miller, Dorie, 33
Miller, Kelly, 18
Miner, Myrtilla, 9
Ming, Robert, 41
Mitchell, Arthur, 31
Mitchell, Charles L., 20
Molleson, Irving C., 35
Moore, Dr. A.M., 24
Moore, Harry T., 38
Moore, Luke C., 45
Moorhead, Scipio, 3
Morris, Robert, 22
Morrow, E.F., 40
Mossell, Sadie T., 27
Motley, Constance Baker, 51
Moton, Robert R., 20, 26, 30
Muhammad, Elijah, 43
Murphy, Carl, 40

Nabrit, James, Jr., 56
Nau, Elias, 2
Nell, William C., 15, 21
Nino, Alonzo Pedro, 1
Nixon, President Richard, 63, 64
Northrup, Solomon, 15

Olive, Pfc. M.L., 53
O'Neil, Frederick, 35
O'Neill, J., 45
Overton, Anthony, 29
Owens, Jesse, 31

Paine, Thomas, 5
Parker, Charlie, 40
Parker, Mack, 42
Parker, Theodore, 8
Payne, Daniel A., Rev., 8

INDEX

Peake, Mary S., 17
Pease, Joachim, 18
Pennington, James W.C., 8, 20
Perry, Erwin S., 50
Perry, H.B., 52
Perry, Robert E., 25
Petersen, Louis, 37
Peterson, Thomas, 20
Phelp-Stokes, Caroline, 25
Pinchback, P.S.B., 13, 21
Plessy v. Ferguson, 24
Poitier, Sidney, 49
"Pompey", 5
Poole, C.F., 44
Powell, Adam Clayton, 35, 43, 54, 59, 60
Powell, James, 50
Price, Leontyne, 40, 43, 52
Prosser, Gabriel, 5, 7
Pushkin, Alexander, 7

Rainbowe, 2
Rainey, Joseph P., 12
Randolph, Asa Philip, 23, 27, 33, 36, 52
Rangle, Charles B., 67
Ray, Charles Bennet, 8
Ray, Charlotte E., 21
Ray, James Earl, 59
Reason, Charles L., 10
Remond, Charles Lenox, 8, 13
Revels, Hiram R., 10, 25
Rice, Dan, 11
Rice, Emmet T., 54
Richardson, S., 39
Riles, Wilson, 66
Rillieux, Norbert, 8
Rivers, Francis E., 29
Roberts, Adelbert H., 27
Roberts, Mrs. Ann, 47
Roberts, Benjamin, 15
Roberts, Needham R., 27
Roberts, William B., 63
Robeson, Paul, 35
Robinson, Bernard W., 33
Robinson, Bill, 37

Robinson, Frank, 44
Robinson, Jackie, 36, 40, 45
Rock, John S., 19
Roosevelt, President Franklin D., 33
Roosevelt, Mrs. F.D., 32
Rowan, Carl T., 43, 48
Rucker, H.A., 24
Rugambwa, Bishop Laurian, 42
Ruggles, David, 8
Rummel, Archbishop J.F., 47
Rush, Benjamin D., 7
Russell, Senator Richard B., 50
Russell, William F. (Bill), 45, 51, 53
Russworm, John, 11

Saible, Jean Baptiste Pointe Du, 3, 4
Salem, Peter, 4
Sampson, Mrs. E., 37
Scarborough, Dr. William S., 27
Scott, Dred, 15, 16
Scott, Emmett J., 26
Scott, Dr. Hugh S., 66
Seale, Bobby, 61
Searles, Joseph L., 63
Sejour, Victor, 10
Sewall, Samuel, 3
Shaw, Robert Gould, 13
Shelly v. Kraemer, 37
Silver, James W., 48
Simms, Hilda, 35
Simpson, Georgiana R., 27
Skinner, Eliot P., 53
Smalls, Robert, 13, 17
Smith v. Allwright, 34
Smith, Bessie, 32
Smith, Charlie, 14
Smith, James McCune, 9, 13
Smith, Marion O., 44
Smith, Tommie, 58
Snowden, Dr. F.M., 39
Spingarn, Arthur B., 50, 52
Spingarn, Joel E., 26, 29
Spottswood, Bishop Stephen G., 66
Staupers, Mabel K., 38
Still, William, 10, 19, 21

Still, William Grant, 24
Stokes, Carl, 56, 62
Stowe, Harriet Beecher, 8
Sullivan, Dr. Leon H., 67
Sutton, Percy, 54
Sumner, Charles, 8

Talbert, Mary B., 27
Tanner, Henry O., 16
Tappan, Arthur, 6
Tarbell, Ida, 29
Taylor, Hobart, Jr., 46, 50
Taylor, Bishop Prince A.T., Jr., 52
Temple, Lewis, 15
Terrell, Dr., Mary Church, 18, 24, 39
Thomas, Franklin A., 61
Thomas, John, 45
Thompson, Jack, 30
Thompson, Pfc. W.H., 38
Thomy, Lafon, 8
Till, Emmet, 40
Tobrias, Channing H.,
Tolon, August, 16
Townsend, James M., 14
Trotter, William M., 25
Truth, Sojourner, 7, 14, 23
Tubman, Harriet, 10, 15, 26
Tucker, William, 1
Turner, Henry MacNeil, 12
Turner, James M., 13
Turner, Nat, 7, 11, 12
Tyler, President, 14

Varick, James, 4
Vesey, Denmark, 10
Victoria, Francisco Xavier de Luna, 2

Walden, A.T., 49
Walden, John Bishop, 12
Walker, David, 6, 11
Walker, Edward G., 20
Walker, Maggie Lena, 20

Walker, Wyatt T., 51
Wallace, Gov. George C., 61, 65
Ward, Samuel Ringgold, 10, 20
Warfield, William, 64
Waring, Judge, 38
Washington, Booker T., 16, 17, 21, 22, 24, 26, 34, 41
Washington, Dinah, 48
Washington, George, 4, 5, 9
Waters, Ethel, 32
Wayne, Anthony, 5
Wayne, Daniel Bishop, 9
Weaver, George L.P., 44
Weaver, Robert C., 43, 45, 52
Well, Ida B., 24
Weston, Dr. M.M., 61
Wharton, Clifton R., 41, 62
Wheatley, Phillis, 3, 5, 6
Whipple, Prince, 5
Whipper, William, 12, 13, 23
White, George L., 21
White, Josh, 61
White, Walter F., 23, 32, 40
Whitman, M., 39
Whitney, Eli, 6
Whittier, John Greenleaf, 12
Wilkins, Ernest J., 39
Wilkins, Roy, 40, 49
Williams, "Bert", 22
Williams, Billy, 44
Williams, Carol, 39
Williams, Daniel Hale, 16, 23, 30
Williams, Frances, 3
Williams, George Washington, 23
Williams, Paul R., 39
Williams, William T.B., 31
Wills, Maury, 47
Woods, Granville T., 16
Woodson, Carter G., 21, 26, 27, 37
Woolman, John, 3
Work, John W., 21
Wright, Louis T., 33
Wright, Richard, 33, 43
Wright, Stephen J., 53

Wright, Theodore S., 13

X, Malcolm, 51

Yergan, Max, 30
Young, Charles Colonel, 19, 26, 27
Young, Whitney, Jr., 50, 67